PowerXL Air Fryer Grill Cookbook:

100 Quick and Easy Recipes for Smart People on a Budget Fry, Grill, Bake, and Roast Your Tasty Meals

TABLE OF CONTENTS

INTRODUCTION

The XL Deep Fryer is an easy way to cook delicious healthy meals. Instead of cooking your meals in oil, this machine uses air to cook. You can cook all kinds of food, even snacks and appetizers. Food cooks quickly and evenly without the need for added oils. Enjoy cooking healthier than ever before.

This amazing appliance is simple to use. Just add the food you wish to cook and turn the 3 burners on. You can fry, grill, bake, roast, and even smoke. The appliance can also be used to boil, steam, freeze, and dehydrate. With Complete Powerxl fryer, you have no restrictions on what you can cook. With the XL Deep Fryer, you can easily make healthy takeout food that would cost you a fortune.

In this cookbook, you will find all the great recipes you ever needed. The cookbook also comes with a free garlic bread recipe.

Benefits of Deep Frying

Air Frying is much better for you than deep frying. Deep frying used a lot of oil and a lot of fat, both of which are bad for you. Air fryers use very little fat, if any at all. A goal of the Complete Powerxl fryer is to cook without the use of any added fat, using air, or any other kind of liquid. This is a revolutionary change in the way you cook. You can enjoy your favorite deep-fried foods without the guilt or the extra pounds.

Air fryers use completely no oils to cook. Air Frying cooks in temperatures between 400-425 degrees (F). This temperature is generally enough to cook a variety of foods without losing taste or texture. You can also roast, bake, grill, smoke and many other things using this appliance. This cookbook will give you all the information you need on how to prepare your food in an easy-to-understand way.

Air frying provides healthier foods than deep frying. Because of this, deep fried foods have a bad reputation. If you enjoy fried foods, then air frying is the way to go. Air frying can give you the taste of deep-fried food with none of the guilt.

Some of the recipes in this cookbook use frozen food. Our frozen recipe section is the best section to be found anywhere. The recipes are simple to make and extremely tasty. Air frying provides healthier frozen foods with ingredients that you can read and understand. Deep frying does not have the same process for making food. The ingredients in deep fried food are unreadable and can be a cause of illness.

Air frying is best for families. Air frying oil is far more cost friendly than deep fried foods. You will spend less money on fats, oils, flour, and grease when you air fry. With Complete Powerxl Air Fryer, you can cook healthier fast food. Air Fryer provides fast and delicious foods. All meals are healthy and tasty. You will always have a delicious meal ready for you and your family.

Complete Powerxl air fryer comes with a lot of additional features. You have a separate temperature control. A feature this air fryer is famous for is the timer. You will enjoy simple deep frys when you have this appliance on hand. The timer will fit perfectly into your routine of dieting and preparing meals. You will never have to fry after work again.

When purchasing this air fryer, you will get lots of additional features. These features include a recipe cookbook and recipes for frozen foods. You will also find a free garlic bread recipe with your purchase. This recipe is offered free of charge. We encourage you to utilize the recipe page for more information. You will also find a 90-day warranty on all our products.

If you are ready to take the plunge and purchase Complete Powerxl Air Fryer, you will be glad you did. A deep-fried food is one of the most popular food items everyone loves. But you will find that air fried food is much more protective of your health. You can place an air fryer in your home and prepare your meals with some tasty recipes.

ESSENTIALS OF POWERXL AIR FRYER GRILL

What is the PowerXL Air Fryer Grill?

A multifunction air fryer and grill, the PowerXL Air Fryer Grill offers a plethora of menu possibilities with up to 70 percent fewer calories from fat than traditional frying.

It features eight cooking presets that let you air fry and grill at the same time, air fry, grill, toast, broil, rotisserie or reheat food with less cooking oil or none at all. It also does not require thawing and can cook food straight from the freezer.

The PowerXL Air Fryer Grill boasts an up to 450-degree superheated air circulation that ensures the food is cooked evenly on all sides, extra crispy on the outside and tenderly juicy on the inside.

The unit heats almost instantly with a smart preheat feature that starts the timer only when it reaches the desired temperature. It also shuts off automatically.

Equipped with two racks, the PowerXL Air Fryer Grill can cook as much as 4.5 times more food than traditionally smaller air fryers. Ideal for cooking meals for the whole family or when hosting a gathering, the large capacity allows the unit to accommodate up to 10 pounds of chicken, a 12-inch round pizza, six toast slices or bagels, or the equivalent load of a 4.5-quart Dutch oven.

The Working Principle

In general, air fryers feature a fan that circulates hot air within its chambers in order to cook food. The hot air radiates from the chamber through the heating elements near the food.

To control the temperature, excess hot air is released through an air inlet on the top and an exhaust at the back of the unit.

Instead of being completely submerged in hot oil, food in air fryers are air-heated to induce the Maillard reaction, resulting in browned food with a distinct aroma and taste.

The PowerXL Air Fryer Grill's fan is equipped with turbo blades that are more powerful than its competitors. These blades are angled strategically in order to distribute heat evenly over the surface of the food. Depending on the kind of food, cooking times are reduced by at least 20 percent in comparison with that of traditional ovens.

It also comes with a non-stick grill plate that creates gorgeous grill marks and chargrill flavor without the use of charcoal or propane.

Step-by-step Procedure of Using It

Operating your PowerXL Air Fryer Grill is a breeze with its easy to assemble parts and accessories and simple control panel. After choosing the desired settings, you can just leave it and forget about it until it is time to eat.

Before using the unit for the first time, read all materials, labels and stickers. Remove all packaging, labels and stickers prior to operation. Hand wash all removable parts and accessories with soapy water.

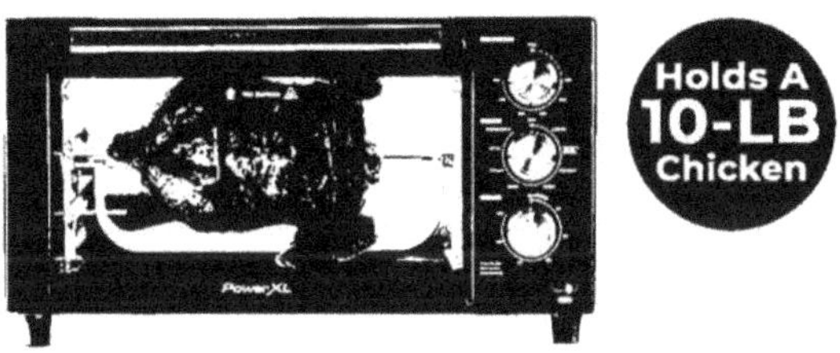

Place the PowerXL Air Fryer Grill on a safe, stable, level, horizontal and heat-resistant surface in an area with good air circulation. Keep the unit away from hot surfaces, other objects or appliances, and combustible materials. It is advisable to plug the unit to a designated outlet.

Carefully assemble the parts and accessories. On the left side of the air fryer's door, you will see guides that indicate the ideal place for the racks and pans. The drip tray should be kept below the heating elements at all times when cooking.

Preheat the unit to allow the manufacturer's protective coating to burn, and then wipe off with a warm moist cloth.

Lightly grease the food before cooking to ensure that it would not stick to the pan or to each other. You may opt to use healthier plant-based oils like avocado and olive. If you are cooking wet food such as marinated meat, pat them dry first to avoid excessive splattering and smoke while cooking.

Avoid overcrowding the food for hot air to circulate effectively and achieve crispy results. Also keep in mind that air fryers cook food faster so follow recommended temperature settings to avoid overcooking or burning.

There are three knobs for: (1)adjusting temperature(up to 450 degrees)and toast darkness options, (2)selecting cooking function (air fry, air fry/grill, pizza/bake, grill, broil, reheat, toast/bagel, rotisserie), and setting the timer(up to 120 minutes).

To make toast, set the toast darkness first and then choose the toast/bagel function. Next, turn the timer knob clockwise past the 20-minute mark, and then rotate counterclockwise to the toast icon.

For the rest of the cooking functions, turn the timer knob past the 20-minute mark before adjusting it to the desired time.

You must select a cooking function for the device to start. When a cooking function and time have been set, the light will turn on. Once the timer expires, the light goes off.

Tips for Care & Maintenance

It is a good practice to visually inspect your PowerXL Air Fryer before each use to make sure that it will function safely and properly. Air fryers may be built to last a long time but just like any other kitchen appliance, you may encounter a few minor and easy-to-fix problems with them from time to time.

Cleaning & Deodorizing

Make sure that the unit is clean before each use. Check the inside for any debris or accumulated dust if you have not been using your unit for some time.

Clean the unit immediately after each use, especially after cooking foods with a pungent smell. Unplug the air fryer and allow it to cool down for at least 30 minutes.

All of the removable parts and accessories are dishwasher safe. If you prefer to handwash, use a mild detergent and soft moist cloth. Do not use abrasive cleaning materials.

Regularly empty the accumulated fat from the bottom of the machine to avoid excessive smoke when cooking.

How to Store It

After cleaning, make sure that the unit and all its parts and components are dry before storing away. Ensure that the unit will be kept in a stable, level and upright position while in storage. Keep it in a cool, dry place.

Frequently Asked Questions (FAQs)

What is unit size and load capacity of the PowerXL Air Fryer Grill?

The product measures 15.1 x 19.3 x 10. 4 inches, with a capacity of 930 cubic inches.

What is the wattage?

1500 watts

What are the accessories that come with the Air Fryer Grill?

The PowerXL Air Fryer Grill has a grill plate, crisper tray, a rotisserie spit set, a baking pan, a drip tray, and an oven/pizza rack. The deluxe unit also includes a non-stick griddle plate and an egg/muffin tray.

Will the PowerXL help me eat healthier?

The PowerXL Air Fryer grill uses hot air instead of oil or butter to produce a crispy brown effect, creating lower calorie alternatives to our favorite fried foods.

What food can I prepare food in PowerXL Air Fryer grill?

You can crisp anything from roasted chicken and steak to potatoes and vegetables. The eight cooking functions can assure you that whether craving classic French fries or corn muffins, your all-in-one air fryer got it all for you.

BREAKFAST

1. Radish Hash Browns

Basic Recipe

Preparation Time: 10 minutes

Cooking Time: 13 minutes

Servings: 4

INGREDIENTS:

- 1 lb. radishes, washed and cut off roots
- 1 tbsp olive oil
- 1/2 tsp paprika

- 1/2 tsp onion powder
- 1/2 tsp garlic powder
- 1 medium onion
- 1/4 tsp pepper
- 3/4 tsp sea salt

DIRECTIONS:

1. Slice onion and radishes using a mandolin slicer.
2. Add sliced onion and radishes in a large mixing bowl and toss with olive oil.
3. Transfer onion and radish slices in air fryer basket and cook at 360 F for 8 minutes Shake basket twice.
4. Return onion and radish slices in a mixing bowl and toss with seasonings.
5. Again, cook onion and radish slices in air fryer basket for 5 minutes at 400 F. Shake the basket halfway through.
6. Serve and enjoy.

NUTRITION: Calories 62 Fat 3.7 g Carbs 7.1 g Protein 1.2 g

2. Vegetable Egg Cups

Basic Recipe

Preparation Time: 10 minutes

Cooking Time: 20 minutes

Servings: 4

INGREDIENTS:

- 4 eggs
- 1 tbsp cilantro, chopped
- 4 tbsp half and half
- 1 cup cheddar cheese, shredded
- 1 cup vegetables, diced
- Pepper
- Salt

DIRECTIONS:

1. Sprinkle four ramekins with cooking spray and set aside.
2. In a mixing bowl, whisk eggs with cilantro, half and half, vegetables, 1/2 cup cheese, pepper, and salt.
3. Pour egg mixture into the four ramekins.
4. Place ramekins in air fryer basket and cook at 300 F for 12 minutes
5. Top with remaining 1/2 cup cheese and cook for 2 minutes more at 400 F.
6. Serve and enjoy.

NUTRITION: Calories 194 Fat 11.5 g Carbs 6 g Protein 13 g

3. Spinach Frittata

Basic Recipe

Preparation Time: 5 minutes

Cooking Time: 8 minutes

Servings: 1

INGREDIENTS:

- 3 eggs
- 1 cup spinach, chopped
- 1 small onion, minced
- 2 tbsp mozzarella cheese, grated
- Pepper
- Salt

DIRECTIONS:

1. Preheat the air fryer to 350 F. Spray air fryer pan with cooking spray.
2. In a bowl, whisk eggs with remaining ingredients until well combined.
3. Pour egg mixture into the prepared pan and place pan in the air fryer basket.
4. Cook frittata for 8 minutes or until set. Serve and enjoy.

NUTRITION: Calories 384 Fat 23.3 g Carbs 10.7 g Protein 34.3 g

4. Omelet Frittata

Basic Recipe

Preparation Time: 10 minutes

Cooking Time: 6 minutes

Servings: 2

INGREDIENTS:

- 3 eggs, lightly beaten
- 2 tbsp cheddar cheese, shredded
- 2 tbsp heavy cream
- 2 mushrooms, sliced
- 1/4 small onion, chopped
- 1/4 bell pepper, diced
- Pepper
- Salt

DIRECTIONS:

1. In a bowl, whisk eggs with cream, vegetables, pepper, and salt.
2. Preheat the air fryer to 400 F.
3. Pour egg mixture into the air fryer pan. Place pan in air fryer basket and cook for 5 minutes
4. Add shredded cheese on top of the frittata and cook for 1 minute more.
5. Serve and enjoy.

NUTRITION: Calories 160 Fat 10 g Carbs 4 g Protein 12 g

5. Cheese Soufflés

Basic Recipe

Preparation Time: 10 minutes

Cooking Time: 6 minutes

Servings: 8

INGREDIENTS:

- 6 large eggs, separated
- 3/4 cup heavy cream
- 1/4 tsp cayenne pepper
- 1/2 tsp xanthan gum
- 1/2 tsp pepper
- 1/4 tsp cream of tartar
- 2 tbsp chives, chopped
- 2 cups cheddar cheese, shredded
- 1 tsp salt

DIRECTIONS:

1. Preheat the air fryer to 325 F.
2. Spray eight ramekins with cooking spray. Set aside.
3. In a bowl, whisk together almond flour, cayenne pepper, pepper, salt, and xanthan gum.
4. Slowly add heavy cream and mix to combine.
5. Whisk in egg yolks, chives, and cheese until well combined.
6. In a large bowl, add egg whites and cream of tartar and beat until stiff peaks form.
7. Fold egg white mixture into the almond flour mixture until combined.
8. Pour mixture into the prepared ramekins. Divide ramekins in batches.
9. Place the first batch of ramekins into the air fryer basket.
10. Cook soufflé for 20 minutes
11. Serve and enjoy.

NUTRITION: Calories 210 Fat 16 g Carbs 1 g Protein 12 g

6. Simple Egg Soufflé

Basic Recipe

Preparation Time: 5 minutes

Cooking Time: 8 minutes

Servings: 2

INGREDIENTS:

- 2 eggs
- 1/4 tsp chili pepper
- 2 tbsp heavy cream
- 1/4 tsp pepper
- 1 tbsp parsley, chopped
- Salt

DIRECTIONS:

1. In a bowl, whisk eggs with remaining gradients.
2. Spray two ramekins with cooking spray.
3. Pour egg mixture into the prepared ramekins and place into the air fryer basket.
4. Cook soufflé at 390 F for 8 minutes
5. Serve and enjoy.

NUTRITION: Calories 116 Fat 10 g Carbs 1.1 g Protein 6 g

7. Vegetable Egg Soufflé

Basic Recipe

Preparation Time: 10 minutes

Cooking Time: 20 minutes

Servings: 4

INGREDIENTS:

- 4 large eggs
- 1 tsp onion powder
- 1 tsp garlic powder
- 1 tsp red pepper, crushed
- 1/2 cup broccoli florets, chopped
- 1/2 cup mushrooms, chopped

DIRECTIONS:

1. Sprinkle four ramekins with cooking spray and set aside.
2. In a bowl, whisk eggs with onion powder, garlic powder, and red pepper.
3. Add mushrooms and broccoli and stir well.
4. Pour egg mixture into the prepared ramekins and place ramekins into the air fryer basket.
5. Cook at 350 F for 15 minutes Make sure soufflé is cooked if soufflé is not cooked then cook for 5 minutes more.
6. Serve and enjoy.

NUTRITION: Calories 91 Fat 5.1 g Carbs 4.7 g Protein 7.4 g

8. Asparagus Frittata

Basic Recipe

Preparation Time: 10 minutes

Cooking Time: 10 minutes

Servings: 4

INGREDIENTS:

- 6 eggs
- 3 mushrooms, sliced
- 10 asparagus, chopped
- 1/4 cup half and half
- 2 tsp butter, melted
- 1 cup mozzarella cheese, shredded
- 1 tsp pepper
- 1 tsp salt

DIRECTIONS:

1. Toss mushrooms and asparagus with melted butter and add into the air fryer basket. Cook mushrooms and asparagus at 350 F for 5 minutes Shake basket twice.
2. Meanwhile, in a bowl, whisk together eggs, half and half, pepper, and salt. Transfer cook mushrooms and asparagus into the air fryer baking dish. Pour egg mixture over mushrooms and asparagus.
3. Place dish in the air fryer and cook at 350 F for 5 minutes or until eggs are set. Slice and serve.

NUTRITION: Calories 211 Fat 13 g Carbs 4 g Protein 16 g

9. Spicy Cauliflower Rice

Basic Recipe

Preparation Time: 10 minutes

Cooking Time: 22 minutes

Servings: 2

INGREDIENTS:

- 1 cauliflower head, cut into florets
- 1/2 tsp cumin
- 1/2 tsp chili powder
- 6 onion spring, chopped
- 2 jalapenos, chopped
- 4 tbsp olive oil
- 1 zucchini, trimmed and cut into cubes
- 1/2 tsp paprika
- 1/2 tsp garlic powder
- 1/2 tsp cayenne pepper
- 1/2 tsp pepper
- 1/2 tsp salt

DIRECTIONS:

1. Preheat the air fryer to 370 F.
2. Add cauliflower florets into the food processor and process until it looks like rice.

3. Transfer cauliflower rice into the air fryer baking pan and Drizzle with half oil.
4. Place pan in the air fryer and cook for 12 minutes, stir halfway through.
5. Heat the remaining oil in a small pan over medium heat.
6. Add zucchini and cook for 5-8 minutes
7. Add onion and jalapenos and cook for 5 minutes
8. Add spices and stir well. Set aside.
9. Add cauliflower rice in the zucchini mixture and stir well.
10. Serve and enjoy.

NUTRITION: Calories 254 Fat 28 g Carbs 12.3 g Protein 4.3 g

10. Broccoli Stuffed Peppers

Basic Recipe

Preparation Time: 10 minutes

Cooking Time: 40 minutes

Servings: 2

INGREDIENTS:

- 4 eggs
- 1/2 cup cheddar cheese, grated
- 2 bell peppers cut in half and remove seeds
- 1/2 tsp garlic powder
- 1 tsp dried thyme
- 1/4 cup feta cheese, crumbled

- 1/2 cup broccoli, cooked
- 1/4 tsp pepper
- 1/2 tsp salt

DIRECTIONS:

1. Preheat the air fryer to 325 F.
2. Stuff feta and broccoli into the bell peppers halved.
3. Beat egg in a bowl with seasoning and pour egg mixture into the pepper halved over feta and broccoli.
4. Place bell pepper halved into the air fryer basket and cook for 35-40 minutes
5. Top with grated cheddar cheese and cook until cheese melted.
6. Serve and enjoy.

NUTRITION: Calories 340 Fat 22 g Carbs 12 g Protein 22 g

11. Zucchini Muffins

Basic Recipe

Preparation Time: 10 minutes

Cooking Time: 20 minutes

Servings: 8

INGREDIENTS:

- 6 eggs
- 4 drops stevia
- 1/4 cup Swerve
- 1/3 cup coconut oil, melted

- 1 cup zucchini, grated
- 3/4 cup coconut flour
- 1/4 tsp ground nutmeg
- 1 tsp ground cinnamon
- 1/2 tsp baking soda

DIRECTIONS:

1. Preheat the air fryer to 325 F.
2. Add all ingredients except zucchini in a bowl and mix well.
3. Add zucchini and stir well.
4. Pour batter into the silicone muffin molds and place into the air fryer basket.
5. Cook muffins for 20 minutes
6. Serve and enjoy.

NUTRITION: Calories 136 Fat 12 g Carbs 1 g Protein 4 g

12. Jalapeno Breakfast Muffins

Preparation Time: 10 minutes

Cooking Time: 15 minutes

Servings: 8

INGREDIENTS:

- 5 eggs
- 1/3 cup coconut oil, melted
- 2 tsp baking powder
- 3 tbsperythritol

- 3 tbsp jalapenos, sliced
- 1/4 cup unsweetened coconut milk
- 2/3 cup coconut flour
- 3/4 tsp sea salt

DIRECTIONS:

1. Preheat the air fryer to 325 F.
2. In a large bowl, mix together coconut flour, baking powder, erythritol, and sea salt.
3. Stir in eggs, jalapenos, coconut milk, and coconut oil until well combined.
4. Pour batter into the silicone muffin molds and place into the air fryer basket.
5. Cook muffins for 15 minutes
6. Serve and enjoy.

NUTRITION: Calories 125 Fat 12 g Carbs 7 g Protein 3 g

13. Zucchini Noodles

Intermediate Recipe

Preparation Time: 10 minutes

Cooking Time: 44 minutes

Servings: 3

INGREDIENTS:

- 1 egg
- 1/2 cup parmesan cheese, grated

- 1/2 cup feta cheese, crumbled
- 1 tbsp thyme
- 1 garlic clove, chopped
- 1 onion, chopped
- 2 medium zucchinis, trimmed and spiralized
- 2 tbsp olive oil
- 1 cup mozzarella cheese, grated
- 1/2 tsp pepper
- 1/2 tsp salt

DIRECTIONS:

1. Preheat the air fryer to 350 F.
2. Add spiralized zucchini and salt in a colander and set aside for 10 minutes. Wash zucchini noodles and pat dry with a paper towel.
3. Heat the oil in a pan over medium heat.Add garlic and onion and sauté for 3-4 minutes
4. Add zucchini noodles and cook for 4-5 minutes or until softened.
5. Add zucchini mixture into the air fryer baking pan. Add egg, thyme, cheeses. Mix well and season.
6. Place pan in the air fryer and cook for 30-35 minutes
7. Serve and enjoy.

NUTRITION: Calories 435 Fat 29 g Carbs 10.4 g Protein 25 g

14. Mushroom Frittata

Basic Recipe

Preparation Time: 10 minutes

Cooking Time: 13 minutes

Servings: 1

INGREDIENTS:

- 1 cup egg whites
- 1 cup spinach, chopped
- 2 mushrooms, sliced
- 2 tbsp parmesan cheese, grated
- Salt

DIRECTIONS:

1. Sprinkle pan with cooking spray and heat over medium heat.Add mushrooms and sauté for 2-3 minutes Add spinach and cook for 1-2 minutes or until wilted.
2. Transfer mushroom spinach mixture into the air fryer pan.Beat egg whites in a mixing bowl until frothy. Season it with a pinch of salt.
3. Pour egg white mixture into the spinach and mushroom mixture and sprinkle with parmesan cheese. Place pan in air fryer basket and cook frittata at 350 F for 8 minutes
4. Slice and serve.

NUTRITION: Calories 176 Fat 3 g Carbs 4 g Protein 31 g

15. Egg Muffins

Basic Recipe

Preparation Time: 10 minutes

Cooking Time: 15 minutes

Servings: 12

INGREDIENTS:

- 9 eggs
- 1/2 cup onion, sliced
- 1 tbsp olive oil
- 8 oz ground sausage
- 1/4 cup coconut milk
- 1/2 tsp oregano
- 1 1/2 cups spinach
- 3/4 cup bell peppers, chopped
- Pepper
- Salt

DIRECTIONS:

1. Preheat the air fryer to 325 F.
2. Add ground sausage in a pan and sauté over medium heat for 5 minutes
3. Add olive oil, oregano, bell pepper, and onion and sauté until onion is translucent.
4. Put spinach to the pan and cook for 30 seconds.
5. Remove pan from heat and set aside.

6. In a mixing bowl, whisk together eggs, coconut milk, pepper, and salt until well beaten.
7. Add sausage and vegetable mixture into the egg mixture and mix well.
8. Pour egg mixture into the silicone muffin molds and place into the air fryer basket. (Cook in batches)
9. Cook muffins for 15 minutes
10. Serve and enjoy.

NUTRITION: Calories 135 Fat 11 g Carbs 1.5 g Protein 8 g

16. Parmesan Sticks

Preparation time: 5 minutes

Cooking time: 15 minutes

Servings: 4

INGREDIENTS:

- ¼ Teaspoon Black Pepper
- 4 Tablespoons Almond Flour
- 1 Egg
- ½ Cup Heavy Cream
- 8 Ounces Parmesan Cheese

DIRECTIONS:

1. Crack your egg into a bowl, beating it. Add in your almond flour and cream, mixing well.
2. Sprinkle your cream mixture with black pepper, whisking well.
3. Cut your cheese into short, thick sticks, and then dip it in the cream mixture. Place these sticks in a plastic bag and place them in the freezer. Let them freeze.
4. Turn your air fryer to 400, and then place your frozen sticks on the air fryer rack, and then cook for eight minutes.

NUTRITION: Calories: 389 Protein: 28.6 Grams Fat: 29.5 Grams Net Carbs: 4.4 Grams

17. Garlic Mozzarella Sticks

Preparation time: 1 hour and 5 minutes

Cooking time: 10 minutes

Servings: 4

INGREDIENTS:

- 1 Tablespoon Italian Seasoning
- 1 Cup Parmesan Cheese
- 8 String Cheeses, Diced
- 2 Eggs, Beaten
- 1 Clove Garlic, Minced

DIRECTIONS:

1. Start by combining your parmesan, garlic and Italian seasoning in a bowl. Dip your cheese into the egg, and mix well.
2. Roll it into your cheese crumbles, and then press the crumbs into the cheese.
3. Place them in the fridge for an hour, and then preheat your air fryer to 375.
4. Spray your air fryer down with oil, and then arrange the cheese strings into the basket. Cook for eight to nine minutes at 365.
5. Allow them to cool for at least five minutes before serving.

NUTRITION: Calories: 80 Protein: 7 Grams Fat: 6.2 Grams Net Carbs: 3 Grams

18. Zucchini Chips

Preparation time: 5 minutes

Cooking time: 20 minutes

Servings: 4

INGREDIENTS:

- 2 Zucchini
- 1 Teaspoon Olive Oil
- 1 Teaspoon Paprika
- Sea Salt to Taste

DIRECTIONS:

1. Preheat your air fryer to 370, and then slice your zucchini.

2. Sprinkle your salt and paprika over the zucchini. Sprinkle them down with oil, and then cook for thirteen minutes.

NUTRITION: Calories: 22 Protein: 1 Gram Fat: 1.1 Grams Net Carbs: 1.9 Grams

19. Pork Rinds

Preparation time: 5 minutes

Cooking time: 10 minutes

Servings: 8

INGREDIENTS:

- ½ Teaspoon Black Pepper
- 1 Teaspoon Chili Flakes
- ½ Teaspoon Sea Salt, Fine
- 1 Teaspoon Olive Oil
- 1 lb. Pork Rinds

DIRECTIONS:

1. Start by heating your air fryer to 365, and then spray it down with olive oil.
2. Place your pork rinds in your air fryer basket, and sprinkle with your seasoning. Mix well, and then cook for seven minutes.
3. Shake gently, and then serve cooled.

NUTRITION: Calories: 329 Protein: 36.5 Grams Fat: 20.8 Grams Net Carbs: 0.1 Grams

20. Roasted Parsnips

Preparation time: 5 minutes

Cooking time: 40 minutes

Servings: 4

INGREDIENTS:

- 2 lbs. Parsnips, Peeled & Cut into Chunks
- 2 Tablespoons Maple Syrup
- 1 Tablespoon Olive Oil
- 1 Tablespoon Parsley Flakes

DIRECTIONS:

1. Start by heating your air fryer to 360, and then add in your ingredients. Make sure that your parsnips are well coated.
2. Cook for forty minutes, and then serve warm.

NUTRITION: Calories: 124 Protein: 4 Grams Fat: 3 Grams Carbs: 7 Grams

21. Honey Roasted Carrots

Preparation time: 5 minutes

Cooking time: 20 minutes

Servings: 4

INGREDIENTS:

- 1 Tablespoon Honey, Raw

- 3 Cups Baby Carrots
- 1 Tablespoon Olive Oil
- Sea Salt & Black Pepper to Taste

DIRECTIONS:

1. Put all of the ingredients in a bowl, then heat your air fryer to 390.
2. Cook for twelve minutes and serve warm.

NUTRITION: Calories: 82 Protein: 1 Gram Fat: 3.2 Grams Carbs: 2.1 Grams

22. Crisp Broccoli

Preparation time: 5 minutes

Cooking time: 20 minutes

Servings: 4

INGREDIENTS:

- 1 Tablespoon Lemon Juice, Fresh
- 2 Teaspoon Olive Oil
- 1 Head Broccoli

DIRECTIONS:

1. Start by rinsing your broccoli and patting it dry. Cut it into florets, and then separate them. Make sure that if you use the stems it's cut into one-inch chunks and peeled.

2. Toss your broccoli pieces with your lemon juice and olive oil until they're well coated. Roast your broccoli in the fryer in batches for ten for fourteen minutes. Each. They should be tender and crisp, and then serve warm.

NUTRITION: Calories: 63 Protein: 4 Grams Fat: 2 Grams Net Carbs: 10 Grams

23. Roasted Bell Pepper

Preparation time: 5 minutes

Cooking time: 20 minutes

Servings: 4

INGREDIENTS:

- 1 Teaspoon Olive Oil
- ½ Teaspoon Thyme
- 4 Cloves Garlic, Minced
- 4 Bell Peppers, Cut into Fourths

DIRECTIONS:

1. Start by putting your peppers in your air fryer basket and drizzling with olive oil. Make sure they're coated well, and then roast for fifteen minutes.
2. Sprinkle with thyme and garlic, roasting for an additional three to five minutes. They should be tender, and serve warm.

NUTRITION: Calories: 36 Protein: 1 Gram Fat: 1 Gram Carbs: 5 Grams

24. Curried Brussels Sprouts

Preparation time: 5 minutes

Cooking time: 25 minutes

Servings: 4

INGREDIENTS:

- 1 lb. Brussel Sprouts, end Trimmed & Halved
- 2 Teaspoons Olive Oil
- 1 Tablespoon Lemon Juice, Fresh
- 3 Teaspoons Curry Powder, Divided

DIRECTIONS:

1. Start by getting gout a large bowl and mix together your olive oil with a teaspoon of curry powder. Toss your Brussel sprouts in, mixing until well coated. Place them in your air fryer basket, roasting for twelve minutes. During this Cooking Time you'll need to shake your basket once.
2. Sprinkle with the remaining curry powder and lemon juice, shaking your basket again. Roast for an additional three to five minutes. Your Brussel sprouts should be crisp and browned. Serve warm.

NUTRITION: Calories: 86 Protein: 4 Grams Fat: 3 Grams Carbs: 12 Grams

25. Garlic Asparagus

Preparation time: 5 minutes

Cooking time: 10 minutes

Servings: 4

INGREDIENTS:

- 1 lb. Asparagus, Rinsed & Trimmed
- 2 Teaspoons Olive Oil
- 3 Cloves Garlic, Minced
- 2 Tablespoons Balsamic Vinegar
- ½ Teaspoon Thyme

DIRECTIONS:

1. Start by getting out a large bowl to toss your asparagus in olive oil before placing your vegetables in the air fryer basket.
2. Sprinkle with garlic before roasting for eight to eleven minutes. Your asparagus should be tender but crisp.
3. Drizzle with thyme and balsamic vinegar before serving warm.

NUTRITION: Calories: 41 Protein: 3 Grams Fat: 1 Gram Carbs: 6 Grams

26. Roasted Garlic

Preparation time: 5 minutes

Cooking time: 30 minutes

Servings: 10

INGREDIENTS:

- 3 whole garlic bulbs, halved
- 3 tablespoons olive oil
- ¼ teaspoon kosher salt

DIRECTIONS:

1. Select the Bake function on the Air Fryer, adjust time to 30 minutes, then press Start/Cancel to heat up.
2. Flavor garlic halves with olive oil and salt.
3. Layer the food tray with parchment paper, then place garlic bulb halves face down onto the food tray.
4. Insert the food tray at a low position in the warmed-up air fryer, then press Start/Cancel to start baking.
5. Flip garlic halves face up after cooking for 20 minutes.
6. Remove garlic halves when done and serve as a side, or make it into a paste to spread with butter over toast.

NUTRITION: Calories 39, Total Fat 4.2g, Total Carbs 0.2g, Protein 0.3g

27. Dehydrated Candied Bacon

Preparation time: 3 hours

Cooking time: 4 hours and 10 minutes

Servings: 4

INGREDIENTS:

- 6 slices bacon

- 3 tablespoons light brown sugar
- 2 tablespoons rice vinegar
- 2 tablespoons chili paste
- 1 tablespoon soy sauce

DIRECTIONS:

1. Mix brown sugar, rice vinegar, chili paste, and soy sauce together in a bowl.
2. Add bacon slices and mix until all are evenly coated.
3. Set aside for up to 3 hours or up until ready to dehydrate.
4. Then put the bacon on the food tray.
5. Set bacon on the air fryer 's wire rack, then insert the rack at mid-position in the air fryer toaster oven.
6. Select the Dehydrate function on the Air Fryer, set time to 4 hours, then press Start.
7. Remove the tray once done baking and let the bacon cool for 5 minutes, then serve.

NUTRITION: Calories 137, Total Fat 8.8g, Total Carbs 6.9g, Protein 7.6g

28. Dehydrated Spiced Orange Slices

Preparation time: 10 minutes

Cooking time: 6 hours

Servings: 3

INGREDIENTS:

- 2 large oranges, cut into ⅛-inch-thick slices
- ½ teaspoon ground star anise
- ½ teaspoon ground cinnamon
- 1 tbsp Choco-hazelnut spread

DIRECTIONS:

1. Dash seasonings on the orange slices.
2. Place into the fry basket, then insert the basket at mid-position in the Air Fryer.
3. Select the Dehydrate function, fix the time to 6 hours and temperature to 140°F, then press Start.
4. Remove once done, and if desired serve with chocolate hazelnut spread.

NUTRITION: Calories 99, Total Fat 2.2g, Total Carbs 18.2g, Protein 1.6g

29. Ranch Kale Chip

Preparation time: 5 minutes

Cooking time: 3 hours

Servings: 2

INGREDIENTS:

- 3 whole kale leaves, cut into 2-inch squares
- 1 tbsp. olive oil
- 1 tbsp. ranch seasoning

DIRECTIONS:

1. In a small bowl, mix the olive oil and ranch seasoning.
2. Mix ranch mixture with kale leaves until all are evenly coated.
3. Put the kale leaves into the fry basket, then insert the fry basket at mid-position in the Air Fryer.
4. Select the Dehydrate function, fix the time to 3 hours and temperature to 140°F, then press Start/Cancel.
5. Remove when done and serve.

NUTRITION: Calories 117, Total Fat 7g, Total Carbs 10.5g, Protein 3g

30. Taco Seasoned Kale Chips

Preparation time: 5 minutes

Cooking time: 3 hours

Servings: 2

INGREDIENTS:

- 3 whole kale leaves, cut into 2-inch squares
- 1 tbsp.olive oil
- 1 tbsp. taco seasoning

DIRECTIONS:

1. Mix taco seasoning and olive oil in a small bowl.
2. Combine taco seasoning mixture with kale leaves until all are evenly coated.

3. Place kale leaves into the fry basket, then insert the fry basket at mid-position in the Air Fryer.
4. Select the Dehydrate function, fix the time to 3 hours and temperature to 140°F, then press Start.
5. Remove when done and serve.

NUTRITION: Calories 125, Total Fat 7g, Total Carbs 12.5g, Protein 3g

POULTRY RECIPES

31. Crispy Air Fryer Butter Chicken

Preparation Time: 5 minutes

Cooking Time: 15 minutes

Servings: 4

INGREDIENTS:

- 2 (8-ounce) boneless, skinless chicken breasts
- 1 sleeve Ritz crackers
- 4 tablespoons (½ stick) cold unsalted butter, cut into 1-tablespoon slices

DIRECTIONS:

1. Preparing the Ingredients. Spray the Cuisinart air fryer basket with olive oil, or spray an air fryer–size baking sheet with olive oil or cooking spray.
2. Dip the chicken breasts in water. Put the crackers in a resealable plastic bag. Using a mallet or your hands, crush the crackers. Place the chicken breasts inside the bag one at a time and coat them with the cracker crumbs.
3. Place the chicken in the greased air fryer basket, or on the greased baking sheet set into the air fryer basket. Put 1 to 2 dabs of butter onto each piece of chicken.
4. Air Frying. Set the temperature of your Cuisinart AF to 370°F. Set the timer and bake for 7 minutes.
5. Using tongs, flip the chicken. Spray the chicken generously with olive oil to avoid uncooked breading. Reset the timer and bake for 7 minutes more.
6. Check that the chicken has reached an internal temperature of 165°F. Add Cooking Time if needed. Using tongs, remove the chicken from the air fryer and serve.

NUTRITION: Calories: 750 Fat: 40g Carbohydrate: 38g Protein: 57g

32. Light and Airy Breaded Chicken Breasts

Preparation Time: 5 minutes

Cooking Time: 15 minutes

Servings: 2

INGREDIENTS:

- 2 large eggs
- 1cup bread crumbs or panko bread crumbs
- 1 teaspoon Italian seasoning
- 4 to 5 tablespoons vegetable oil
- 2 boneless, skinless, chicken breasts

DIRECTIONS:

1. Preparing the Ingredients. Preheat the Cuisinart air fryer to 370°F. Spray the Cuisinart air fryer basket with olive oil or cooking spray. In a small bowl, whisk the eggs until frothy. In a separate small mixing bowl, mix together the bread crumbs, Italian seasoning, and oil. Dip the chicken in the egg mixture, then in the bread crumb mixture. Place the chicken directly into the greased air fryer basket, or on the greased baking sheet set into the basket.
2. Air Frying. Spray the chicken generously and thoroughly with olive oil to avoid powdery, uncooked breading. Set the timer and fry for 7 minutes. Using tongs, flip the chicken and generously spray it with olive oil. Reset the timer and fry for 7 minutes more. Check that the chicken has reached an internal temperature of 165°F. Add Cooking Time if needed. Once the chicken is fully cooked, use tongs to remove it from the air fryer and serve.

NUTRITION: Calories: 833 Fat: 46g Carbohydrate: 40g Protein: 65g

33. Chicken Fillets, Brie & Ham

Preparation Time: 5 minutes

Cooking Time: 15 minutes

Servings: 4

INGREDIENTS:

- 2 Large Chicken Fillets
- Freshly Ground Black Pepper
- 4 Small Slices of Brie (Or your cheese of choice)
- 1 Tbsp Freshly Chopped Chives
- 4 Slices Cured Ham

DIRECTIONS:

1. Preparing the Ingredients. Slice the fillets into four and make incisions as you would for a hamburger bun. Leave a little "hinge" uncut at the back. Season the inside and pop some brie and chives in there. Close them, and wrap them each in a slice of ham. Brush with oil and pop them into the basket.
2. Air Frying. Heat your fryer to 350° F. Roast the little parcels until they look tasty (15 min)

NUTRITION: Calories: 850 Carbs: 43 g Fat: 50 g Protein: 76 g

34. Air Fryer Cornish Hen

Preparation Time: 5 minutes

Cooking Time: 30 minutes

Servings: 2

INGREDIENTS:

- 2 tablespoons Montreal chicken seasoning
- 1 (1½- to 2-pound) Cornish hen

DIRECTIONS:

1. Preheat the Cuisinart air fryer to 390°F. Rub the seasoning over the chicken, coating it thoroughly.
2. Put the chicken in the basket. Set the timer and roast for 15 minutes.
3. Flip the chicken and cook for another 15 minutes. Check that the chicken has reached an internal temperature of 165°F. Add Cooking Time if needed.

NUTRITION: Calories: 520 Fat: 36g Carbohydrate: 0g Protein: 45g

35. Air Fried Turkey Wings

Preparation Time: 5 minutes

Cooking Time: 26 minutes

Servings: 4

INGREDIENTS:

- 2 pounds turkey wings
- 3 tablespoons olive oil or sesame oil
- 3 to 4 tablespoons chicken rub

DIRECTIONS:

1. Put the turkey wings in a large mixing bowl. Pour the olive oil into the bowl and add the rub. Using your hands, rub the oil mixture over the turkey wings. Place the turkey wings in the air fryer basket.
2. Fix the temperature of your Air Fryer to 380°F. Set the timer and roast for 13 minutes.
3. Using tongs, flip the wings. Reset the timer and roast for 13 minutes more. Remove the turkey wings from the air fryer, plate, and serve.

NUTRITION: Calories: 521 Fat: 34g Carbohydrate: 4g Protein: 52g

36. Chicken-Fried Steak Supreme

Preparation Time: 10 minutes

Cooking Time: 30 minutes

Servings: 8

INGREDIENTS:

- ½ pound beef-bottom round, sliced into strips
- 1 cup of breadcrumbs
- 2 medium-sized eggs
- Pinch of salt and pepper
- ½ tablespoon of ground thyme

DIRECTIONS:

1. Preparing the Ingredients. Cover the basket of the Air fryer with a layer of tin foil, leaving the edges open to allow air to

flow through the basket. Preheat the air fryer to 350 degrees. In a bowl, whisk the eggs until fluffy and until the yolks and whites are fully combined, and set aside. In a separate bowl, mix the breadcrumbs, thyme, salt and pepper, and set aside. One by one, dip each piece of raw steak into the bowl with dry ingredients, coating all sidesthen submerge into the bowl with wet ingredients, then dip again into the dry ingredients. This double coating will ensure an extra crisp air fry. Lay the coated steak pieces on the foil covering the air-fryer basket, in a single flat layer.

2. Air Frying. Set the Cuisinart air fryer timer for 15 minutes. After 15 minutes, the air fryer will turn off and the steak should be mid-way cooked and the breaded coating starting to brown. Using tongs, turn each piece of steak over to ensure a full all-over fry. Reset the air fryer to 320 ° for 15 minutes. After 15 minutes, when the air fryer shuts off, remove the fried steak strips using tongs and set on a serving plate. Eat once cool enough to handle and enjoy.

NUTRITION: Calories: 421 Fat: 26g Carbs: 8g Protein: 46g

37. Caesar Marinated Grilled Chicken

Preparation Time: 10 minutes

Cooking Time: 25 minutes

Servings: 4

INGREDIENTS:

- ¼ cup crouton
- 1 teaspoon lemon zest. Form into ovals, skewer and grill.
- 1/2 cup Parmesan
- 1/4 cup breadcrumbs
- 1-pound ground chicken
- 2 tablespoons Caesar dressing and more for drizzling
- 2-4 romaine leaves

DIRECTIONS:

1. In a shallow dish, mix well chicken, 2 tablespoons Caesar dressing, parmesan, and breadcrumbs. Mix well with hands. Form into 1-inch oval patties. Thread chicken pieces in skewers. Place on skewer rack in air fryer.
2. For 12 minutes, cook on 360°F. Halfway through Cooking Time, turnover skewers. If needed, cook in batches. Serve on a bed of lettuce and sprinkle with croutons and extra dressing.

NUTRITION: Calories: 342 Fat: 12g Carbs: 8g Protein: 36g

38. Cheesy Chicken Tenders

Preparation Time: 10 minutes

Cooking Time: 30 minutes

Servings: 4

INGREDIENTS:

- 1 large white meat chicken breast
- 1 cup of breadcrumbs

- 2 medium-sized eggs
- Pinch of salt and pepper
- 1 tablespoon of grated or powdered parmesan cheese

DIRECTIONS:

1. Cover the basket of the Air fryer with a layer of tin foil, leaving the edges open to allow air to flow through the basket. Preheat the Cuisinart air fryer to 350 degrees. In a bowl, whisk the eggs until fluffy and until the yolks and whites are fully combined, and set aside. In a separate bowl, mixt he breadcrumbs, parmesan, salt and pepper, and set aside. One by one, dip each piece of raw chicken into the bowl with dry ingredients, coating all sidesthen submerge into the bowl with wet ingredients, then dip again into the dry ingredients. Put the coated chicken pieces on the foil covering the Air fryer basket, in a single flat layer.
2. Set the Cuisinart air fryer timer for 15 minutes. After 15 minutes, the air fryer will turn off and the chicken should be mid-way cooked and the breaded coating starting to brown. Flip each piece of chicken over to ensure a full all over fry. Reset the Cuisinart air fryer to 320 degrees for another 15 minutes. After 15 minutes, when the air fryer shuts off, remove the fried chicken strips using tongs and set on a serving plate. Eat once cool enough to handle, and enjoy.

NUTRITION: Calories: 278 Fat: 15g Protein:29g; Sugar:7g

39. Minty Chicken-Fried Pork Chops

Preparation Time: 10 minutes

Cooking Time: 30 minutes

Servings: 4

INGREDIENTS:

- 4medium-sized pork chops
- 1 cup of breadcrumbs
- 2 medium-sized eggs
- Pinch of salt and pepper
- ½ tablespoon of mint, either dried and groundor fresh, rinsed, and finely chopped

DIRECTIONS:

1. Preparing the Ingredients. Cover the basket of the Air fryer with a layer of tin foil, leaving the edges open to allow air to flow through the basket. Preheat the Cuisinart air fryer to 350 degrees. In a mixing bowl, whisk the eggs until fluffy and until the yolks and whites are fully combined, and set aside. In a separate bowl, mix the breadcrumbs, mint, salt and pepper, and set aside. One by one, dip each raw pork chop into the bowl with dry ingredients, coating all sidesthen submerge into the bowl with wet ingredients, then dip again into the dry ingredients. Lay the coated pork chops on the foil covering the Air fryer basket, in a single flat layer.
2. Air Frying. Set the Cuisinart air fryer timer for 15 minutes. After 15 minutes, the Air fryer will turn off and the pork should be mid-way cooked and the breaded coating

starting to brown. Using tongs, turn each piece of steak over to ensure a full all-over fry. Reset the Cuisinart air fryer to 320 degrees for 15 minutes. After 15 minutes remove the fried pork chops using tongs and set on a serving plate.

NUTRITION: Calories: 262 Fat: 17g Carbs: 7g Protein: 32g

40. Bacon Lovers' Stuffed Chicken

Preparation Time: 10 minutes

Cooking Time: 20 minutes

Servings: 4

INGREDIENTS:

- 4 (5-ounce) boneless, skinless chicken breasts, sliced into ¼ inch thick
- 2 packages Boursin cheese
- 8 slices thin-cut bacon or beef bacon
- Sprig of fresh cilantro, for garnish

DIRECTIONS:

1. Preparing the Ingredients. Spray the Cuisinart air fryer basket with avocado oil. Preheat the Cuisinart air fryer to 400°F. Put one of the chicken breasts on a cutting board. With a sharp knife held parallel to the cutting board, make a 1-inch-wide incision at the top of the breast. Carefully cut into the breast to form a large pocket, leaving a ½-inch border along the sides and bottom. Repeat with the other 3 chicken breasts. Snip the

corner of a large resealable plastic bag to form a ¾-inch hole. Place the Boursin cheese in the bag and pipe the cheese into the pockets in the chicken breasts, dividing the cheese evenly among them. Wrap 2 slices of bacon around each chicken breast and secure the ends with toothpicks.

2. Air Frying. Place the bacon-wrapped chicken in the Cuisinart air fryer basket and cook until the bacon is crisp and the chicken's internal temperature reaches 165°F, about 18 to 20 minutes, flipping after 10 minutes. Garnish with a sprig of cilantro before serving, if desired.

NUTRITION: Calories: 446 Fat: 17g Carbs: 13g Protein: 36g

41. Air Fryer Turkey Breast

Preparation Time: 5 minutes

Cooking Time: 60 minutes

Servings: 6

INGREDIENTS:

- Pepper and salt
- 1 oven-ready turkey breast
- Turkey seasonings of choice

DIRECTIONS:

1. Preheat the Cuisinart air fryer to 350 degrees.
2. Season turkey with pepper, salt, and other desired seasonings.
3. Place turkey in air fryer basket.

4. Set temperature to 350°F, and set time to 60 minutes. Cook 60 minutes. The meat should be at 165 degrees when done. Allow to rest 10-15 minutes before slicing. Enjoy.

NUTRITION: Calories: 212 Fat: 12g Protein:24g Sugar:0g

42. Mustard Chicken Tenders

Preparation Time: 5 minutes

Cooking Time: 20 minutes

Servings: 4

INGREDIENTS:

- ½ C. coconut flour
- 1 tbsp. spicy brown mustard
- 2 beaten eggs
- 1 pound of chicken tenders

DIRECTIONS:

1. Season tenders with pepper and salt.
2. Place a thin layer of mustard onto tenders and then dredge in flour and dip in egg.
3. Add to the Air fryer, set temperature to 390°F, and set time to 20 minutes.

NUTRITION: Calories: 346 Fat: 10g Carbs: 12g Protein: 31g

43. Chicken Meatballs

Preparation Time: 5 minutes

Cooking Time: 15 minutes

Servings: 2

INGREDIENTS:

- ½ lb chicken breast
- 1 tbsp of garlic
- 1 tbsp of onion
- ½ chicken broth
- 1 tbsp of oatmeal, whole wheat flour or of your choice

DIRECTIONS:

1. Place all of the ingredients in a food processor and beat well until well mixed and ground.
2. If you don't have a food processor, ask the butcher to grind it and then add the other ingredients, mixing well.
3. Make balls and place them in the Air Fryer basket.
4. Program the Air Fryer for 15 minutes at 400°F.
5. Half the time shake the basket so that the meatballs loosen and fry evenly.

NUTRITION: Calories: 45 Carbohydrates: 1.94g Fat: 1.57g Protein: 5.43g Sugar: 0.41g Cholesterol: 23m

44. Homemade Breaded Nugget In Doritos

Preparation Time: 10 minutes

Cooking Time: 15 minutes

Servings: 4

INGREDIENTS:

- ½ lb. boneless, skinless chicken breast
- ¼ lb. Doritos snack
- 1 cup of wheat flour
- 1 egg
- Salt, garlic and black pepper to taste.

DIRECTIONS:

1. Cut the chicken breast in the width direction, 1 to 1.5 cm thick, so that it is already shaped like pips.
2. Season with salt, garlic, black pepper to taste and some other seasonings if desired.
3. You can also season with those seasonings or powdered onion soup.
4. Put the Doritos snack in a food processor or blender and beat until everything is crumbled, but don't beat too much, you don't want flour.
5. Now bread, passing the pieces of chicken breast first in the wheat flour, then in the beaten eggs and finally in the Doritos, without leaving the excess flour, eggs or Doritos.
6. Place the seeds in the Air Fryer basket and program for 15 minutes at 400°F, and half the time they brown evenly.

NUTRITION: Calories: 42 Carbohydrates: 1.65g Fat: 1.44g Protein: 5.29g Sugar: 0.1g Cholesterol: 20mg

45. Chicken Breast

Preparation Time: 30 minutes

Cooking Time: 25 minutes

Servings: 6

INGREDIENTS:

- 1 lb. diced clean chicken breast
- ½ lemon
- Smoked paprika to taste
- Black pepper or chili powder, to taste
- Salt to taste

DIRECTIONS:

1. Flavor the chicken with salt, paprika and pepper and marinate.
2. Store in Air fryer and turn on for 15 minutes at 350°F.
3. Turn the chicken over and raise the temperature to 200°C, and turn the Air Fryer on for another 5 minutes or until golden.
4. Serve immediately.

NUTRITION: Calories: 124 Carbohydrates: 0g Fat: 1.4g Protein: 26.1g Sugar: 0g Cholesterol: 66mg

MEAT RECIPES

46. Simple Beef Sirloin Roast

Preparation Time: 10 minutes

Cooking Time: 50 minutes

Servings: 8

INGREDIENTS:

- 2½ pounds sirloin roast
- Salt and ground black pepper, as required

DIRECTIONS:

1. Rub the roast with salt and black pepper generously.
2. Insert the rotisserie rod through the roast.
3. Insert the rotisserie forks, one on each side of the rod to secure the rod to the chicken.

4. Arrange the drip pan in the bottom of Instant Vortex Plus Air Fryer Oven cooking chamber.
5. Select "Roast" and then adjust the temperature to 350 degrees F.
6. Set the timer for 50 minutes and press the "Start".
7. When the display shows "Add Food" press the red lever down and load the left side of the rod into the Vortex.
8. Now, slide the rod's left side into the groove along the metal bar so it doesn't move.
9. Then, close the door and touch "Rotate".
10. When cooking time is complete, press the red lever to release the rod.
11. Remove from the Vortex and place the roast onto a platter for about 10 minutes before slicing.
12. With a sharp knife, cut the roast into desired sized slices and serve.

NUTRITION: Calories 201 Total Fat 8.8 g Saturated Fat 3.1 g Cholesterol 94 mg Sodium 88 mg Total Carbs 0 g Fiber 0 g Sugar 0 g Protein 28.9 g

47. Seasoned Beef Roast

Preparation Time: 10 minutes

Cooking Time: 45 minutes

Servings: 10

INGREDIENTS:

- 3 pounds beef top roast
- 1 tablespoon olive oil
- 2 tablespoons Montreal steak seasoning

DIRECTIONS:

1. Coat the roast with oil and then rub with the seasoning generously.
2. With kitchen twines, tie the roast to keep it compact.
3. Arrange the roast onto the cooking tray.
4. Arrange the drip pan in the bottom of Instant Vortex Plus Air Fryer Oven cooking chamber.
5. Select "Air Fry" and then adjust the temperature to 360 degrees F.
6. Set the timer for 45 minutes and press the "Start".
7. When the display shows "Add Food" insert the cooking tray in the center position.
8. When the display shows "Turn Food" do nothing.
9. When cooking time is complete, remove the tray from Vortex and place the roast onto a platter for about 10 minutes before slicing.
10. With a sharp knife, cut the roast into desired sized slices and serve.

NUTRITION: Calories 269 Total Fat 9.9 g Saturated Fat 3.4 g Cholesterol 122 mg Sodium 538 mg

48. Bacon Wrapped Filet Mignon

Preparation Time: 10 minutes

Cooking Time: 15 minutes

Servings: 2

INGREDIENTS:

- 2 bacon slices
- 2 (4-ounce) filet mignon
- Salt and ground black pepper, as required
- Olive oil cooking spray

DIRECTIONS:

1. Wrap 1 bacon slice around each filet mignon and secure with toothpicks.
2. Season the filets with the salt and black pepper lightly.
3. Arrange the filet mignon onto a coking rack and spray with cooking spray.
4. Arrange the drip pan in the bottom of Instant Vortex Plus Air Fryer Oven cooking chamber.
5. Select "Air Fry" and then adjust the temperature to 375 degrees F.
6. Set the timer for 15 minutes and press the "Start".
7. When the display shows "Add Food" insert the cooking rack in the center position.
8. When the display shows "Turn Food" turn the filets.
9. When cooking time is complete, remove the rack from Vortex and serve hot.

NUTRITION: Calories 360 Total Fat 19.6 g Saturated Fat 6.8 g Cholesterol 108 mg Sodium 737 mg Total Carbs 0.4 g Fiber 0 g Sugar 0 g Protein 42.6 g

49. Beef Burgers

Preparation Time: 15 minutes

Cooking Time: 18 minutes

Servings: 4

INGREDIENTS:

- For Burgers:
- 1-pound ground beef
- ½ cup panko breadcrumbs
- ¼ cup onion, chopped finely
- 3 tablespoons Dijon mustard
- 3 teaspoons low-sodium soy sauce
- 2 teaspoons fresh rosemary, chopped finely
- Salt, to taste
- For Topping:
- 2 tablespoons Dijon mustard
- 1 tablespoon brown sugar
- 1 teaspoon soy sauce
- 4 Gruyere cheese slices

DIRECTIONS:

1. In a large bowl, add all the ingredients and mix until well combined.
2. Make 4 equal-sized patties from the mixture.
3. Arrange the patties onto a cooking tray.
4. Arrange the drip pan in the bottom of Instant Vortex Plus Air Fryer Oven cooking chamber.
5. Select "Air Fry" and then adjust the temperature to 370 degrees F.
6. Set the timer for 15 minutes and press the "Start".
7. When the display shows "Add Food" insert the cooking rack in the center position.
8. When the display shows "Turn Food" turn the burgers.
9. Meanwhile, for sauce: in a small bowl, add the mustard, brown sugar and soy sauce and mix well.
10. When cooking time is complete, remove the tray from Vortex and coat the burgers with the sauce.
11. Top each burger with 1 cheese slice.
12. Return the tray to the cooking chamber and select "Broil".
13. Set the timer for 3 minutes and press the "Start".
14. When cooking time is complete, remove the tray from Vortex and serve hot.

NUTRITION: Calories 402 Total Fat 18 g Saturated Fat 8.5 g Cholesterol 133mg Sodium 651 mg Total Carbs 6.3 g Fiber 0.8 g Sugar 3 g Protein 44.4 g

50. Beef Jerky

Preparation Time: 15 minutes

Cooking Time: 3 hours

Servings: 4

INGREDIENTS:

- 1½ pounds beef round, trimmed
- ½ cup Worcestershire sauce
- ½ cup low-sodium soy sauce
- 2 teaspoons honey
- 1 teaspoon liquid smoke
- 2 teaspoons onion powder
- ½ teaspoon red pepper flakes
- Ground black pepper, as required

DIRECTIONS:

1. In a zip-top bag, place the beef and freeze for 1-2 hours to firm up.
2. Place the meat onto a cutting board and cut against the grain into 1/8-¼-inch strips.
3. In a large bowl, add the remaining ingredients and mix until well combined.
4. Add the steak slices and coat with the mixture generously.
5. Refrigerate to marinate for about 4-6 hours.
6. Remove the beef slices from bowl and with paper towels, pat dry them.

7. Divide the steak strips onto the cooking trays and arrange in an even layer.
8. Select "Dehydrate" and then adjust the temperature to 160 degrees F.
9. Set the timer for 3 hours and press the "Start".
10. When the display shows "Add Food" insert 1 tray in the top position and another in the center position.
11. After 1½ hours, switch the position of cooking trays.
12. Meanwhile, in a small pan, add the remaining ingredients over medium heat and cook for about 10 minutes, stirring occasionally.
13. When cooking time is complete, remove the trays from Vortex.

NUTRITION: Calories 372 Total Fat 10.7 g Saturated Fat 4 g Cholesterol 152 mg Sodium 2000 mg Total Carbs 12 g Fiber 0.2 g Sugar 11.3 g Protein 53.8 g

51. Sweet & Spicy Meatballs

Preparation Time: 20 minutes

Cooking Time: 30 minutes

Servings: 8

INGREDIENTS:

- For Meatballs:
- 2 pounds lean ground beef
- 2/3 cup quick-cooking oats
- ½ cup Ritz crackers, crushed

- 1 (5-ounce) can evaporated milk
- 2 large eggs, beaten lightly
- 1 teaspoon honey
- 1 tablespoon dried onion, minced
- 1 teaspoon garlic powder
- 1 teaspoon ground cumin
- Salt and ground black pepper, as required
- For Sauce:
- 1/3 cup orange marmalade
- 1/3 cup honey
- 1/3 cup brown sugar
- 2 tablespoons cornstarch
- 2 tablespoons soy sauce
- 1-2 tablespoons hot sauce
- 1 tablespoon Worcestershire sauce

DIRECTIONS:

1. For meatballs: in a large bowl, add all the ingredients and mix until well combined.
2. Make 1½-inch balls from the mixture.
3. Arrange half of the meatballs onto a cooking tray in a single layer.
4. Arrange the drip pan in the bottom of Instant Vortex Plus Air Fryer Oven cooking chamber.
5. Select "Air Fry" and then adjust the temperature to 380 degrees F.

6. Set the timer for 15 minutes and press the "Start".
7. When the display shows "Add Food" insert the cooking tray in the center position.
8. When the display shows "Turn Food" turn the meatballs.
9. When cooking time is complete, remove the tray from Vortex.
10. Repeat with the remaining meatballs.
11. Meanwhile, for sauce: in a small pan, add all the ingredients over medium heat and cook until thickened, stirring continuously.
12. Serve the meatballs with the topping of sauce.

NUTRITION: Calories 411 Total Fat 11.1 g Saturated Fat 4.1 g Cholesterol 153 mg Sodium 448 mg Total Carbs 38.8 g Fiber 1 g Sugar 28.1 g Protein 38.9 g

52. Spiced Pork Shoulder

Preparation Time: 15 minutes

Cooking Time: 55 minutes

Servings: 6

INGREDIENTS:

- 1 teaspoon ground cumin
- 1 teaspoon cayenne pepper
- 1 teaspoon garlic powder
- Salt and ground black pepper, as required
- 2 pounds skin-on pork shoulder

DIRECTIONS:

1. In a small bowl, mix together the spices, salt and black pepper.
2. Arrange the pork shoulder onto a cutting board, skin-side down.
3. Season the inner side of pork shoulder with salt and black pepper.
4. With kitchen twines, tie the pork shoulder into a long round cylinder shape.
5. Season the outer side of pork shoulder with spice mixture.
6. Insert the rotisserie rod through the pork shoulder.
7. Insert the rotisserie forks, one on each side of the rod to secure the pork shoulder.
8. Arrange the drip pan in the bottom of Instant Vortex Plus Air Fryer Oven cooking chamber.
9. Select "Roast" and then adjust the temperature to 350 degrees F.
10. Set the timer for 55 minutes and press the "Start".
11. When the display shows "Add Food" press the red lever down and load the left side of the rod into the Vortex.
12. Now, slide the rod's left side into the groove along the metal bar so it doesn't move.
13. Then, close the door and touch "Rotate".
14. When cooking time is complete, press the red lever to release the rod.
15. Remove the pork from Vortex and place onto a platter for about 10 minutes before slicing.

16. With a sharp knife, cut the pork shoulder into desired sized slices and serve.

NUTRITION: Calories 445 Total Fat 32.5 g Saturated Fat 11.9 g Cholesterol 136 mg Sodium 131 mg Total Carbs 0.7 g Fiber 0.2 g Sugar 0.2 g Protein 35.4 g

53. Seasoned Pork Tenderloin

Preparation Time: 10 minutes

Cooking Time: 45 minutes

Servings: 5

INGREDIENTS:

- 1½ pounds pork tenderloin
- 2-3 tablespoons BBQ pork seasoning

Directions:

1. Rub the pork with seasoning generously.
2. Insert the rotisserie rod through the pork tenderloin.
3. Insert the rotisserie forks, one on each side of the rod to secure the pork tenderloin.
4. Arrange the drip pan in the bottom of Instant Vortex Plus Air Fryer Oven cooking chamber.
5. Select "Roast" and then adjust the temperature to 360 degrees F.
6. Set the timer for 45 minutes and press the "Start".

7. When the display shows "Add Food" press the red lever down and load the left side of the rod into the Vortex.
8. Now, slide the rod's left side into the groove along the metal bar so it doesn't move.
9. Then, close the door and touch "Rotate".
10. When cooking time is complete, press the red lever to release the rod.
11. Remove the pork from Vortex and place onto a platter for about 10 minutes before slicing.
12. With a sharp knife, cut the roast into desired sized slices and serve.

NUTRITION: Calories 195 Total Fat 4.8 g Saturated Fat 1.6 g Cholesterol 99 mg Sodium 116 mg Total Carbs 0 g Fiber 0 g Sugar 0 g Protein 35.6 g

54. Garlicky Pork Tenderloin

Preparation Time: 15 minutes

Cooking Time: 20 minutes

Servings: 5

INGREDIENTS:

- 1½ pounds pork tenderloin
- Nonstick cooking spray
- 2 small heads roasted garlic
- Salt and ground black pepper, as required

DIRECTIONS:

1. Lightly, spray all the sides of pork with cooking spray and then, season with salt and black pepper.
2. Now, rub the pork with roasted garlic.
3. Arrange the roast onto the lightly greased cooking tray.
4. Arrange the drip pan in the bottom of Instant Vortex Plus Air Fryer Oven cooking chamber.
5. Select "Air Fry" and then adjust the temperature to 400 degrees F.
6. Set the timer for 20 minutes and press the "Start".
7. When the display shows "Add Food" insert the cooking tray in the center position.
8. When the display shows "Turn Food" turn the pork.
9. When cooking time is complete, remove the tray from Vortex and place the roast onto a platter for about 10 minutes before slicing.
10. With a sharp knife, cut the roast into desired sized slices and serve.

NUTRITION: Calories 202 Total Fat 4.8 g Saturated Fat 1.6 g Cholesterol 99 mg Sodium 109 mg Total Carbs 1.7 g Fiber 0.1 g Sugar 0.1 g Protein 35.9 g

55. Glazed Pork Tenderloin

Preparation Time: 15 minutes

Cooking Time: 20 minutes

Servings: 3

INGREDIENTS:

- 1-pound pork tenderloin
- 2 tablespoons Sriracha
- 2 tablespoons honey
- Salt, as required

DIRECTIONS:

1. Insert the rotisserie rod through the pork tenderloin.
2. Insert the rotisserie forks, one on each side of the rod to secure the pork tenderloin.
3. In a small bowl, add the Sriracha, honey and salt and mix well.
4. Brush the pork tenderloin with honey mixture evenly.
5. Arrange the drip pan in the bottom of Instant Vortex Plus Air Fryer Oven cooking chamber.
6. Select "Air Fry" and then adjust the temperature to 350 degrees F.
7. Set the timer for 20 minutes and press the "Start".
8. When the display shows "Add Food" press the red lever down and load the left side of the rod into the Vortex.
9. Now, slide the rod's left side into the groove along the metal bar so it doesn't move.
10. Then, close the door and touch "Rotate".
11. When cooking time is complete, press the red lever to release the rod.

12. Remove the pork from Vortex and place onto a platter for about 10 minutes before slicing.
13. With a sharp knife, cut the roast into desired sized slices and serve.

NUTRITION: Calories 269 Total Fat 5.3 g Saturated Fat 1.8 g Cholesterol 110 mg Sodium 207 mg

Total Carbs 13.5 g Fiber 0 g Sugar 11.6 g Protein 39.7 g

56. Honey Mustard Pork Tenderloin

Preparation Time: 15 minutes

Cooking Time: 25 minutes

Servings: 3

INGREDIENTS:

- 1-pound pork tenderloin
- 1 tablespoon garlic, minced
- 2 tablespoons soy sauce
- 2 tablespoons honey
- 1 tablespoon Dijon mustard
- 1 tablespoon grain mustard
- 1 teaspoon Sriracha sauce

DIRECTIONS:

1. In a large bowl, add all the ingredients except pork and mix well.
2. Add the pork tenderloin and coat with the mixture generously.

3. Refrigerate to marinate for 2-3 hours.
4. Remove the pork tenderloin from bowl, reserving the marinade.
5. Place the pork tenderloin onto the lightly greased cooking tray.
6. Arrange the drip pan in the bottom of Instant Vortex Plus Air Fryer Oven cooking chamber.
7. Select "Air Fry" and then adjust the temperature to 380 degrees F.
8. Set the timer for 25 minutes and press the "Start".
9. When the display shows "Add Food" insert the cooking tray in the center position.
10. When the display shows "Turn Food" turn the pork and oat with the reserved marinade.
11. When cooking time is complete, remove the tray from Vortex and place the pork tenderloin onto a platter for about 10 minutes before slicing.
12. With a sharp knife, cut the pork tenderloin into desired sized slices and serve.

NUTRITION: Calories 277 Total Fat 5.7 g Saturated Fat 1.8 g Cholesterol 110 mg Sodium 782 mg Total Carbs 14.2 g Fiber 0.4 g Sugar 11.8 g Protein 40.7 g

57. Seasoned Pork Chops

Preparation Time: 10 minutes

Cooking Time: 12 minutes

Servings: 4

INGREDIENTS:

- 4 (6-ounce) boneless pork chops
- 2 tablespoons pork rub
- 1 tablespoon olive oil

DIRECTIONS:

1. Coat both sides of the pork chops with the oil and then, rub with the pork rub.
2. Place the pork chops onto the lightly greased cooking tray.
3. Arrange the drip pan in the bottom of Instant Vortex Plus Air Fryer Oven cooking chamber.
4. Select "Air Fry" and then adjust the temperature to 400 degrees F.
5. Set the timer for 12 minutes and press the "Start".
6. When the display shows "Add Food" insert the cooking tray in the center position.
7. When the display shows "Turn Food" turn the pork chops.
8. When cooking time is complete, remove the tray from Vortex and serve hot.

NUTRITION: Calories 285 Total Fat 9.5 g Saturated Fat 2.5 g Cholesterol 124 mg Sodium 262 mg Total Carbs 1.5 g Fiber 0 g Sugar 0.8 g Protein 44.5 g

58. Breaded Pork Chops

Preparation Time: 15 minutes

Cooking Time: 28 minutes

Servings: 2

INGREDIENTS:

- 2 (5-ounce) boneless pork chops
- 1 cup buttermilk
- ½ cup flour
- 1 teaspoon garlic powder
- Salt and ground black pepper, as required
- Olive oil cooking spray

DIRECTIONS:

1. In a bowl, place the chops and buttermilk and refrigerate, covered for about 12 hours.
2. Remove the chops from the bowl of buttermilk, discarding the buttermilk.
3. In a shallow dish, mix together the flour, garlic powder, salt, and black pepper.
4. Coat the chops with flour mixture generously.
5. Place the pork chops onto the cooking tray and spray with the cooking spray.
6. Arrange the drip pan in the bottom of Instant Vortex Plus Air Fryer Oven cooking chamber.
7. Select "Air Fry" and then adjust the temperature to 380 degrees F.
8. Set the timer for 28 minutes and press the "Start".

9. When the display shows "Add Food" insert the cooking tray in the center position.
10. When the display shows "Turn Food" turn the pork chops.
11. When cooking time is complete, remove the tray from Vortex and serve hot.

NUTRITION: Calories 370 Total Fat 6.4 g Saturated Fat 2.4 g Cholesterol 108 mg Sodium 288 mg

Total Carbs 30.7 g Fiber 1 g Sugar 6.3 g Protein 44.6 g

59. Crusted Rack Of Lamb

Preparation Time: 15 minutes

Cooking Time: 19 minutes

Servings: 4

INGREDIENTS:

- 1 rack of lamb, trimmed all fat and frenched
- Salt and ground black pepper, as required
- 1/3 cup pistachios, chopped finely
- 2 tablespoons panko breadcrumbs
- 2 teaspoons fresh thyme, chopped finely
- 1 teaspoon fresh rosemary, chopped finely
- 1 tablespoon butter, melted
- 1 tablespoon Dijon mustard

DIRECTIONS:

1. Insert the rotisserie rod through the rack on the meaty side of the ribs, right next to the bone.
2. Insert the rotisserie forks, one on each side of the rod to secure the rack.
3. Season the rack with salt and black pepper evenly.
4. Arrange the drip pan in the bottom of Instant Vortex Plus Air Fryer Oven cooking chamber.
5. Select “Air Fry” and then adjust the temperature to 380 degrees F.
6. Set the timer for 12 minutes and press the “Start”.
7. When the display shows “Add Food” press the red lever down and load the left side of the rod into the Vortex.
8. Now, slide the rod’s left side into the groove along the metal bar so it doesn't move.
9. Then, close the door and touch “Rotate”.
10. Meanwhile, in a small bowl, mix together the remaining ingredients except the mustard.
11. When cooking time is complete, press the red lever to release the rod.
12. Remove the rack from Vortex and brush the meaty side with the mustard.
13. Then, coat the pistachio mixture on all sides of the rack and press firmly.
14. Now, place the rack of lamb onto the cooking tray, meat side up.
15. Select “Air Fry” and adjust the temperature to 380 degrees F.
16. Set the timer for 7 minutes and press the “Start”.

17. When the display shows "Add Food" insert the cooking tray in the center position.
18. When the display shows "Turn Food" do nothing.
19. When cooking time is complete, remove the tray from Vortex and place the rack onto a cutting board for at least 10 minutes.
20. Cut the rack into individual chops and serve.

NUTRITION: Calories 824 Total Fat 39.3 g Saturated Fat 14.2 g Cholesterol 233 mg Sodium 373 mg Total Carbs 10.3 g Fiber 1.2 g Sugar 0.2 g Protein 72 g

60. Lamb Burgers

Preparation Time: 15 minutes

Cooking Time: 8 minutes

Servings: 6

INGREDIENTS:

- 2 pounds ground lamb
- 1 tablespoon onion powder
- Salt and ground black pepper, as required

DIRECTIONS:

1. In a bowl, add all the ingredients and mix well.
2. Make 6 equal-sized patties from the mixture.
3. Arrange the patties onto a cooking tray.
4. Arrange the drip pan in the bottom of Instant Vortex Plus Air Fryer Oven cooking chamber.

5. Select "Air Fry" and then adjust the temperature to 360 degrees F.
6. Set the timer for 8 minutes and press the "Start".
7. When the display shows "Add Food" insert the cooking rack in the center position.
8. When the display shows "Turn Food" turn the burgers.
9. When cooking time is complete, remove the tray from Vortex and serve hot.

NUTRITION: Calories 285 Total Fat 11.1 g Saturated Fat 4 g Cholesterol 136 mg Sodium 143 mg Total Carbs 0.9 g Fiber 0.1 g Sugar 0.4 g Protein 42.6 g

SEAFOOD

61. Shrimp, Zucchini and Cherry Tomato Sauce

Preparation Time: 5 minutes

Cooking Time: 30 minutes

Servings: 4

INGREDIENTS:

- 2 zucchinis
- 300 shrimp
- 7 cherry tomatoes
- Salt and pepper to taste
- 1 clove garlic

DIRECTION:

1. Pour the oil in the air fryer, add the garlic clove and diced zucchini.
2. Cook for 15 minutes at 1500C.
3. Add the shrimp and the pieces of tomato, salt, and spices.
4. Cook for another 5 to 10 minutes or until the shrimp water evaporates.

NUTRITION: Calories 214.3 Fat 8.6g Carbohydrate 7.8g Sugars 4.8g Protein 27.0g Cholesterol 232.7mg

62. Salmon with Pistachio Bark

Preparation Time: 10 minutes

Cooking Time: 30 minutes

Servings: 4

INGREDIENTS:

- 600 g salmon fillet
- 50g pistachios
- Salt to taste

DIRECTION:

1. Put the parchment paper on the bottom of the air fryer basket and place the salmon fillet in it (it can be cooked whole or already divided into four portions).

2. Cut the pistachios in thick piecesgrease the top of the fish, salt (little because the pistachios are already salted) and cover everything with the pistachios.
3. Set the air fryer to 1800C and simmer for 25 minutes.

NUTRITION: Calories 371.7 Fat 21.8 g Carbohydrate 9.4 g Sugars 2.2g Protein 34.7 g Cholesterol 80.5 mg

63. Salted Marinated Salmon

Preparation Time: 10 minutes

Cooking Time: 30 minutes

Servings: 4

INGREDIENTS:

- 500g salmon fillet
- 1 kg coarse salt

DIRECTION:

1. Place the baking paper on the air fryer basket and the salmon on top (skin side up) covered with coarse salt.
2. Set the air fryer to 1500C.
3. Cook everything for 25 to 30 minutes. At the end of cooking, remove the salt from the fish and serve with a drizzle of oil.

NUTRITION: Calories 290 Fat 13g Carbohydrates 3g Fiber 0g Protein 40g Cholesterol 196mg

64. Sautéed Trout with Almonds

Preparation Time: 35 minutes

Cooking Time: 20 minutes

Servings: 4

INGREDIENTS:

- 700 g salmon trout
- 15 black peppercorns
- Dill leaves to taste
- 30g almonds
- Salt to taste

DIRECTION:

1. Cut the trout into cubes and marinate it for half an hour with the rest of the ingredients (except salt).
2. Cook in air fryer for 17 minutes at 1600C. Pour a drizzle of oil and serve.

NUTRITION: Calories 238.5 Fat 20.1 g Carbohydrate 11.5 g Sugars 1.0 g Protein4.0 g Cholesterol 45.9 mg

65. Rabas

Preparation Time: 5 minutes

Cooking Time: 12 minutes

Servings: 4

INGREDIENTS:

- 16 rabas
- 1 egg
- Breadcrumbs
- Salt, pepper, sweet paprika

DIRECTION:

1. Put the rabas in the air fryer to boil for 2 minutes.
2. Remove and dry well.
3. Beat the egg and season to taste. You can put salt, pepper and sweet paprika. Place in the egg.
4. Bread with breadcrumbs. Place in sticks.

NUTRITION: Calories 356 Fat 18g Carbohydrates 5 g Protein 34g

66. Honey Glazed Salmon

Preparation Time: 10 minutes

Cooking Time: 8 minutes

Servings: 2

INGREDIENTS:

- 2 (6-oz.) salmon fillets
- Salt, as required
- 2 tablespoons honey

DIRECTIONS:

1. Sprinkle the salmon fillets with salt and then, coat with honey.
2. Press "Power Button" of Air Fry Oven and turn the dial to select the "Air Fry" mode.
3. Press the Time button and again turn the dial to set the Cooking Time to 8 minutes.
4. Now push the Temp button and rotate the dial to set the temperature at 355 degrees F.
5. Press "Start/Pause" button to start.
6. When the unit beeps to show that it is preheated, open the lid.
7. Arrange the salmon fillets in greased "Air Fry Basket" and insert in the oven.
8. Serve hot.

NUTRITION: Calories 289 Fat 10.5 g Carbs 17.3 g Protein 33.1 g

67. Sweet & Sour Glazed Salmon

Preparation Time: 12 minutes

Cooking Time: 20 minutes

Servings: 2

INGREDIENTS:

- 1/3 cup soy sauce
- 1/3 cup honey
- 3 teaspoons rice wine vinegar
- 1 teaspoon water
- 4 (3½-oz.) salmon fillets

DIRECTIONS:

1. Mix the soy sauce, honey, vinegar, and water together in a bowl.
2. In another small bowl, reserve about half of the mixture.
3. Add salmon fillets in the remaining mixture and coat well.
4. Cover the bowl and refrigerate to marinate for about 2 hours.
5. Press "Power Button" of Air Fry Oven and turn the dial to select the "Air Fry" mode.
6. Press the Time button and again turn the dial to set the Cooking Time to 12 minutes.
7. Now push the Temp button and rotate the dial to set the temperature at 355 degrees F.
8. Press "Start/Pause" button to start.
9. When the unit beeps to show that it is preheated, open the lid.
10. Arrange the salmon fillets in greased "Air Fry Basket" and insert in the oven.
11. Flip the salmon fillets once halfway through and coat with the reserved marinade after every 3 minutes.
12. Serve hot.

NUTRITION: Calories 462 Fat 12.3 g Carbs 49.8 g Protein 41.3 g

68. Ranch Tilapia

Preparation Time: 15 minutes

Cooking Time: 13 minutes

Servings: 4

INGREDIENTS:

- ¾ cup cornflakes, crushed
- 1 (1-oz.) packet dry ranch-style dressing mix
- 2½ tablespoons vegetable oil
- 2 eggs
- 4 (6-oz.) tilapia fillets

DIRECTIONS:

1. In a shallow bowl, beat the eggs.
2. In another bowl, add the cornflakes, ranch dressing, and oil and mix until a crumbly mixture form.
3. Dip the fish fillets into egg and then, coat with the breadcrumbs mixture.
4. Press "Power Button" of Air Fry Oven and turn the dial to select the "Air Fry" mode.
5. Press the Time button and again turn the dial to set the Cooking Time to 13 minutes.
6. Now push the Temp button and rotate the dial to set the temperature at 356 degrees F.
7. Press "Start/Pause" button to start.
8. When the unit beeps to show that it is preheated, open the lid.
9. Arrange the tilapia fillets in greased "Air Fry Basket" and insert in the oven.
10. Serve hot.

NUTRITION: Calories 267 Fat 12.2 g Carbs 5.1 g Protein 34.9 g

69. Breaded Flounder

Preparation Time: 15 minutes

Cooking Time: 12 minutes

Servings: 3

INGREDIENTS:

- 1 egg
- 1 cup dry breadcrumbs
- ¼ cup vegetable oil
- 3 (6-oz.) flounder fillets
- 1 lemon, sliced

DIRECTIONS

1. In a shallow bowl, beat the egg
2. In another bowl, add the breadcrumbs and oil and mix until crumbly mixture is formed.
3. Dip flounder fillets into the beaten egg and then, coat with the breadcrumb mixture.
4. Press "Power Button" of Air Fry Oven and turn the dial to select the "Air Fry" mode.
5. Press the Time button and again turn the dial to set the Cooking Time to 12 minutes.
6. Now push the Temp button and rotate the dial to set the temperature at 356 degrees F.
7. Press "Start/Pause" button to start.
8. When the unit beeps to show that it is preheated, open the lid.

9. Arrange the flounder fillets in greased "Air Fry Basket" and insert in the oven.
10. Plate with lemon slices and serve hot.

NUTRITION: Calories 524 Total Fat 24.2 g Saturated Fat 5.1 g Cholesterol 170 mg Sodium 463 mg Total Carbs 26.5 g Fiber 1.5 g Sugar 2.5 g Protein 47.8g

70. Simple Haddock

Preparation Time: 15 minutes

Cooking Time: 8 minutes

Servings: 2

INGREDIENTS:

- 2 (6-oz.) haddock fillets
- 1 tablespoon olive oil
- Salt and ground black pepper, as required

DIRECTIONS

1. Coat the fish fillets with oil and then, sprinkle with salt and black pepper.
2. Press "Power Button" of Air Fry Oven and turn the dial to select the "Air Fry" mode.
3. Press the Time button and again turn the dial to set the Cooking Time to 8 minutes.

4. Now push the Temp button and rotate the dial to set the temperature at 355 degrees F.
5. Press “Start/Pause” button to start.
6. When the unit beeps to show that it is preheated, open the lid.
7. Arrange the haddock fillets in greased “Air Fry Basket” and insert in the oven.
8. Serve hot.

NUTRITION: Calories 251 Total Fat 8.6 g Saturated Fat 1.3 g Cholesterol 126 mg Sodium 226 mg Total Carbs 0 g Fiber 0 g Sugar 0 g Protein 41.2 g

71. Breaded Hake

Preparation Time: 15 minutes

Cooking Time: 12 minutes

Servings: 4

INGREDIENTS:

- 1 egg
- 4 oz. breadcrumbs
- 2 tablespoons vegetable oil
- 4 (6-oz.) hake fillets
- 1 lemon, cut into wedges

DIRECTIONS

1. In a shallow bowl, whisk the egg.

2. In another bowl, add the breadcrumbs, and oil and mix until a crumbly mixture forms.
3. Dip fish fillets into the egg and then, coat with the bread crumbs mixture.
4. Press "Power Button" of Air Fry Oven and turn the dial to select the "Air Fry" mode.
5. Press the Time button and again turn the dial to set the Cooking Time to 12 minutes.
6. Now push the Temp button and rotate the dial to set the temperature at 350 degrees F.
7. Press "Start/Pause" button to start.
8. When the unit beeps to show that it is preheated, open the lid.
9. Arrange the hake fillets in greased "Air Fry Basket" and insert in the oven.
10. Serve hot.

NUTRITION: Calories 297 Total Fat 10.6 g Saturated Fat 2 g Cholesterol 89 mg Sodium 439 mg Total Carbs 22 g Fiber 1.4 g Sugar 1.9 g Protein 29.2 g

72. Sesame Seeds Coated Tuna

Preparation Time: 15 minutes

Cooking Time: 6 minutes

Servings: 2

INGREDIENTS:

- 1 egg white

- ¼ cup white sesame seeds
- 1 tablespoon black sesame seeds
- Salt and ground black pepper, as required
- 2 (6-oz.) tuna steaks

DIRECTIONS

1. In a bowl, beat the egg white.
2. In another bowl, mix together the sesame seeds, salt, and black pepper.
3. Dip the tuna steaks into egg white and then, coat with the sesame seeds mixture.
4. Press "Power Button" of Air Fry Oven and turn the dial to select the "Air Fry" mode.
5. Press the Time button and again turn the dial to set the Cooking Time to 6 minutes.
6. Now push the Temp button and rotate the dial to set the temperature at 400 degrees F.
7. Press "Start/Pause" button to start.
8. When the unit beeps to show that it is preheated, open the lid.
9. Arrange the tuna steaks in greased "Air Fry Basket" and insert in the oven.
10. Flip the tuna steaks once halfway through.
11. Serve hot.

NUTRITION: Calories 450 Total Fat 21.9 g Saturated Fat 4.3 g Cholesterol 83 mg Sodium 182 mg Total Carbs 5.4 g Fiber 2.7 g Sugar 0.2 g Protein 56.7 g

73. Cheese and Ham Patties

Preparation Time: 10 minutes

Cooking Time: 10 minutes

Servings: 4

INGREDIENTS:

- 1 puff pastry sheet
- 4 handfuls mozzarella cheese, grated
- 4 teaspoons mustard
- 8 ham slices, chopped

DIRECTIONS:

1. Spread out puff pastry on a clean surface and cut it in 12 squares.
2. Divide cheese, ham, and mustard on half of them, top with the other halves, and seal the edges.
3. Place all the patties in your air fryer's basket and cook at 370 degrees F for 10 minutes.
4. Divide the patties between plates and serve.

NUTRITION: Calories 212, Fat 12, Fiber 7, Carbs 14, Protein 8

74. Air-Fried Seafood

Preparation Time: 10 minutes

Cooking Time: 10 minutes

Servings: 4

INGREDIENTS:

- 1 lb. fresh scallops, mussels, fish fillets, prawns, shrimp
- 2 eggs, lightly beaten
- Salt and black pepper
- 1 cup breadcrumbs mixed with the zest of 1 lemon
- Cooking spray

DIRECTIONS:

1. Clean the seafood as needed.
2. Dip each piece into the eggand season with salt and pepper.
3. Coat in the crumbs and spray with oil.
4. Arrange into the air fryer and cook for 6 minutes at 4000 F. turning once halfway through.
5. Serve and Enjoy!

NUTRITION: Calories: 133 Protein: 17.4 grams Fat: 3.1 grams Carbohydrates: 8.2 grams

75. Fish with Chips

Preparation Time: 5 minutes

Cooking Time: 20 minutes

Servings: 2

INGREDIENTS:

- 1 cod fillet (6 ounces)
- 3 cups salt
- 3 cups vinegar-flavored kettle cooked chips
- ¼ cup buttermilk
- salt and pepper to taste

DIRECTIONS:

1. Mix to combine the buttermilk, pepper, and salt in a bowl. Put the cod and leave to soak for 5 minutes
2. Put the chips in a food processor and process until crushed. Transfer to a shallow bowl. Coat the fillet with the crushed chips.
3. Put the coated fillet in the air frying basket. Cook for 12 minutes at 4000 F.
4. Serve and Enjoy!

NUTRITION: Calories: 646 Protein: 41 grams Fat: 33 grams Carbohydrates: 48 grams

76. Crumbly Fishcakes

Preparation Time: 5 minutes

Cooking Time: 10 minutes

Servings: 4

INGREDIENTS:

- 8 oz. salmon, cooked

- 1 ½ oz. potatoes, mashed
- A handful of parsley, chopped
- Zest of 1 lemon
- 1 ¾ oz. plain flour

DIRECTIONS:

1. Carefully flakes the salmon. In a bowl, mix flaked salmon, zest, capers, dill, and mashed potatoes.
2. From small cakes using the mixture and dust the cakes with flourrefrigerate for 60 minutes.
3. Preheat your air fryer to 3500 F. and cook the cakes for 7 minutes. Serve chilled.

NUTRITION: Calories: 210 Protein: 10 grams Fat: 7 grams Carbohydrates: 25 grams

77. Bacon Wrapped Shrimp

Preparation Time: 10 minutes

Cooking Time: 20 minutes

Servings: 4

INGREDIENTS:

- 16 thin slices of bacon
- 16 pieces of tiger shrimp (peeled and deveined)

DIRECTIONS:

1. With a slice of bacon, wrap each shrimp. Put all the finished pieces in tray and chill for 20 minutes.
2. Arrange the bacon-wrapped shrimp in the air frying basket. Cook for 7 minutes at 3900 F. Transfer to a plate lined with paper towels to drain before serving.

NUTRITION: Calories: 436 Protein: 32 grams Fat: 41.01 grams Carbohydrates: 0.8 grams

78. Crab Legs

Preparation Time: 10 minutes

Cooking Time: 10 minutes

Servings: 4

INGREDIENTS:

- 3 lb. crab legs
- ¼ cup salted butter, melted and divided
- ½ lemon, juiced
- ¼ tsp. garlic powder

DIRECTIONS:

1. In a bowl, toss the crab legs and two tablespoons of the melted butter together. Place the crab legs in the basket of the fryer.
2. Cook at 400°F for fifteen minutes, giving the basket a good shake halfway through.
3. Combine the remaining butter with the lemon juice and garlic powder.

4. Crack open the cooked crab legs and remove the meat. Serve with the butter dip on the side, and enjoy!

NUTRITION: Calories 272, Fat 19, Fiber 9, Carbs 18, Protein 12

79. Fish Sticks

Preparation Time: 5 minutes

Cooking Time: 10 minutes

Servings: 4

INGREDIENTS:

- 1 lb. whitefish
- 2 tbsp. Dijon mustard
- ¼ cup mayonnaise
- 1 ½ cup pork rinds, finely ground
- ¾ tsp. Cajun seasoning

DIRECTIONS:

1. Place the fish on a tissue to dry it off, then cut it up into slices about two inches thick.
2. In one bowl, combine the mustard and mayonnaise, and in another, the Cajun seasoning and pork rinds.
3. Coat the fish firstly in the mayo-mustard mixture, then in the Cajun-pork rind mixture. Give each slice a shake to remove any surplus. Then place the fish sticks in the basket of the air flyer.
4. Cook at 400°F for five minutes. Turn the fish sticks over and cook for another five minutes on the other side.

5. Serve warm with a dipping sauce of your choosing and enjoy.

NUTRITION: Calories 212, Fat 12, Fiber 7, Carbs 14, Protein 8

80. Crusty Pesto Salmon

Preparation Time: 5 minutes

Cooking Time: 10 minutes

Servings: 2

INGREDIENTS:

- ¼ cup almonds, roughly chopped
- ¼ cup pesto
- 2 x 4-oz. salmon fillets
- 2 tbsp. unsalted butter, melted

DIRECTIONS:

1. Mix the almonds and pesto together.
2. Place the salmon fillets in a round baking dish, roughly six inches in diameter.
3. Brush the fillets with butter, followed by the pesto mixture, ensuring to coat both the top and bottom. Put the baking dish inside the fryer.
4. Cook for twelve minutes at 390°F.
5. The salmon is ready when it flakes easily when prodded with a fork. Serve warm.

NUTRITION: Calories 354 Fat 21 Carbs 23 Protein 19

DESSERTS

81. Sweet Peach Wedges

Preparation Time: 10 minutes

Cooking Time: 8 hours

Servings: 4

INGREDIENTS:

- 3 peaches, cut and remove pits and sliced
- 1/2 cup fresh lemon juice

DIRECTIONS:

1. Add lemon juice and peach slices into the bowl and toss well.
2. Arrange peach slices on instant vortex air fryer oven rack and dehydrate at 135 F for 6-8 hours.
3. Serve and enjoy.

NUTRITION: Calories: 52 Protein: 1.3 g. Fat: 0.5 g. Carbs: 11.1 g.

82. Air Fryer Oreo Cookies

Preparation Time: 5 minutes

Cooking Time: 5 minutes

Servings: 9

INGREDIENTS:

- Pancake Mix: ½ cup
- Water: ½ cup
- Cooking spray
- Chocolate sandwich cookies: 9 (e.g. Oreo)
- Confectioners' sugar: 1 tablespoon, or to taste

DIRECTIONS:

1. Blend the pancake mixture with the water until well mixed.
2. Line the parchment paper on the basket of an air fryer. Spray nonstick cooking spray on parchment paper. Dip each cookie into the mixture of the pancake and place it in the basket. Make sure they do not touchif possible, cook in batches.
3. The air fryer is preheated to 400 degrees F (200 degrees C). Add basket and cook for 4 to 5 minutesflip until golden brown, 2 to 3 more minutes. Sprinkle the sugar over the cookies and serve.

NUTRITION: Calories: 77 Protein: 1.2 g. Fat: 2.1 g. Carbs: 13.7 g.

83. Air Fried Butter Cake

Preparation Time: 10 minutes

Cooking Time: 15 minutes

Servings: 4

INGREDIENTS:

- 7 Tablespoons of butter, at ambient temperature
- White sugar: ¼ cup plus 2 tablespoons
- All-purpose flour: 1 ⅔ cups
- Salt: 1 pinch or to taste
- Milk: 6 tablespoons

DIRECTIONS:

1. Preheat an air fryer to 350 F (180 C). Spray the cooking spray on a tiny fluted tube pan.
2. Take a large bowl and add ¼ cup butter and 2 tablespoons of sugar in it.
3. Take an electric mixer to beat the sugar and butter until smooth and fluffy. Stir in salt and flour. Stir in the milk and thoroughly combine batter. Move batter to the prepared saucepanuse a spoon back to level the surface.
4. Place the pan inside the basket of the air fryer. Set the timer within 15 minutes. Bake the batter until a toothpick comes out clean when inserted into the cake.
5. Turn the cake out of the saucepan and allow it to cool for about five minutes.

NUTRITION: Calories: 470 Protein: 7.9 g .Fat: 22.4 g. Carbs: 59.7 g.

84. Air Fryer S'mores

Preparation Time: 5 minutes

Cooking Time: 3 minutes

Servings: 4

INGREDIENTS:

- Four graham crackers (each half split to make 2 squares, for a total of 8 squares)
- 8 Squares of Hershey's chocolate bar, broken into squares
- 4 Marshmallows

DIRECTIONS:

1. Take deliberate steps. Air-fryers use hot air for cooking food. Marshmallows are light and fluffy, and this should keep the marshmallows from flying around the basket if you follow these steps.
2. Put 4 squares of graham crackers on a basket of the air fryer.
3. Place 2 squares of chocolate bars on each cracker.
4. Place back the basket in the air fryer and fry on air at 390 °F for 1 minute. It is barely long enough for the chocolate to melt. Remove basket from air fryer.
5. Top with a marshmallow over each cracker. Throw the marshmallow down a little bit into the melted chocolate. This will help to make the marshmallow stay over the chocolate.

6. Put back the basket in the air fryer and fry at 390 °F for 2 minutes. (The marshmallows should be puffed up and browned at the tops.)
7. Using tongs to carefully remove each cracker from the basket of the air fryer and place it on a platter. Top each marshmallow with another square of graham crackers.
8. Enjoy it right away!

NUTRITION: Calories: 200 Protein: 2.6 g .Fat: 3.1 g .Carbs: 15.7 g.

85. Peanut Butter Cookies

Preparation Time: 2 minutes

Cooking Time: 5 minutes

Servings: 10

INGREDIENTS:

- Peanut Butter: 1 cup
- Sugar: 1 cup
- 1 Egg

DIRECTIONS:

1. Blend all of the ingredients with a hand mixer.
2. Spray trays of air fryer with canola oil. (Alternatively, parchment paper can also be used, but it will take longer to cook your cookies)
3. Set the air fryer temperature to 350 degrees and preheat it.

4. Place rounded dough balls onto air fryer trays. Press down softly with the back of a fork.
5. Place air fryer tray in your air fryer in the middle place. Cook for five minutes.
6. Use milk to serve with cookies.

NUTRITION: Calories: 236 Protein: 6 g .Fat: 13 g Carbs: 26 g.

86. Sweet Pear Stew

Preparation Time: 10 minutes

Cooking Time: 15 minutes

Servings: 4

INGREDIENTS:

- 4 pears, cored and cut into wedges
- 1 tsp vanilla
- 1/4 cup apple juice
- 2 cups grapes, halved

DIRECTIONS:

1. Put all of the ingredients in the inner pot of air fryer and stir well.
2. Seal pot and cook on high for 15 minutes.
3. As soon as the cooking is done, let it release pressure naturally for 10 minutes then release remaining using quick release. Remove lid.
4. Stir and serve.

NUTRITION: Calories: 162 Protein: 1.1 g. Fat: 0.5 g .Carbs: 41.6 g.

87. Vanilla Apple Compote

Preparation Time: 10 minutes

Cooking Time: 15 minutes

Servings: 6

INGREDIENTS:

- 3 cups apples, cored and cubed
- 1 tsp vanilla
- 3/4 cup coconut sugar
- 1 cup of water
- 2 tbsp fresh lime juice

DIRECTIONS:

1. Put all of the ingredients in the inner pot of air fryer and stir well.
2. Seal pot and cook on high for 15 minutes.
3. As soon as the cooking is done, let it release pressure naturally for 10 minutes then release remaining using quick release. Remove lid.
4. Stir and serve.

NUTRITION: Calories: 76 Protein: 0.5 g. Fat: 0.2 g. Carbs: 19.1 g.

88. Apple Dates Mix

Preparation Time: 10 minutes

Cooking Time: 15 minutes

Servings: 4

INGREDIENTS:

- 4 apples, cored and cut into chunks
- 1 tsp vanilla
- 1 tsp cinnamon
- 1/2 cup dates, pitted
- 1 1/2 cups apple juice

DIRECTIONS:

1. Put all of the ingredients in the inner pot of air fryer and stir well.
2. Seal and cook on high for 15 minutes.
3. As soon as the cooking is done, let it release pressure naturally for 10 minutes then release remaining using quick release. Remove lid.
4. Stir and serve.

NUTRITION: Calories: 226 Protein: 1.3 g. Fat: 0.6 g. Carbs: 58.6 g.

89. Chocolate Rice

Preparation Time: 10 minutes

Cooking Time: 20 minutes

Servings: 4

INGREDIENTS:

- 1 cup of rice
- 1 tbsp cocoa powder
- 2 tbsp maple syrup
- 2 cups almond milk

DIRECTIONS:

1. Put all of the ingredients in the inner pot of air fryer and stir well.
2. Seal pot and cook on high for 20 minutes.
3. As soon as the cooking is done, let it release pressure naturally for 10 minutes then release remaining using quick release. Remove lid.
4. Stir and serve.

NUTRITION: Calories: 474 Protein: 6.3 g .Fat: 29.1 g .Carbs: 51.1 g.

90. Raisins Cinnamon Peaches

Preparation Time: 10 minutes

Cooking Time: 15 minutes

Servings: 4

INGREDIENTS:

- 4 peaches, cored and cut into chunks
- 1 tsp vanilla
- 1 tsp cinnamon
- 1/2 cup raisins
- 1 cup of water

DIRECTIONS:

1. Put all of the ingredients in the inner pot of air fryer and stir well.
2. Seal pot and cook on high for 15 minutes.
3. As soon as the cooking is done, let it release pressure naturally for 10 minutes then release remaining using quick release. Remove lid.
4. Stir and serve.

NUTRITION: Calories: 118 Protein: 2 g .Fat: 0.5 g. Carbs: 29 g.

91. Lemon Pear Compote

Preparation Time: 10 minutes

Cooking Time: 15 minutes

Servings: 6

INGREDIENTS:

- 3 cups pears, cored and cut into chunks
- 1 tsp vanilla
- 1 tsp liquid stevia
- 1 tbsp lemon zest, grated
- 2 tbsp lemon juice

DIRECTIONS:

1. Put all of the ingredients in the inner pot of air fryer and stir well.
2. Seal pot and cook on high for 15 minutes.
3. As soon as the cooking is done, let it release pressure naturally for 10 minutes then release remaining using quick release. Remove lid.
4. Stir and serve.

NUTRITION: Calories: 50 Protein: 0.4 g .Fat: 0.2 g .Carbs: 12.7 g.

92. Strawberry Stew

Preparation Time: 10 minutes

Cooking Time: 15 minutes

Servings: 4

INGREDIENTS:

- 12 oz fresh strawberries, sliced
- 1 tsp vanilla
- 1 1/2 cups water
- 1 tsp liquid stevia
- 2 tbsp lime juice

DIRECTIONS:

1. Put all of the ingredients in the inner pot of air fryer and stir well.
2. Seal pot and cook on high for 15 minutes.

3. As soon as the cooking is done, let it release pressure naturally for 10 minutes then release remaining using quick release. Remove lid.
4. Stir and serve.

NUTRITION: Calories: 36 Protein: 0.7 g.Fat: 0.3 g.Carbs: 8.5 g.

93. Walnut Apple Pear Mix

Preparation Time: 10 minutes

Cooking Time: 10 minutes

Servings: 4

INGREDIENTS:

- 2 apples, cored and cut into wedges
- 1/2 tsp vanilla
- 1 cup apple juice
- 2 tbsp walnuts, chopped
- 2 apples, cored and cut into wedges

DIRECTIONS:

1. Put all of the ingredients in the inner pot of air fryer and stir well.
2. Seal pot and cook on high for 10 minutes.
3. As soon as the cooking is done, let it release pressure naturally for 10 minutes then release remaining using quick release. Remove lid.
4. Serve and enjoy.

NUTRITION: Calories: 132 Protein: 1.3 g. Fat: 2.6 g. Carbs: 28.3 g.

94. Cinnamon Pear Jam

Preparation Time: 10 minutes

Cooking Time: 4 minutes

Servings: 12

INGREDIENTS:

- 8 pears, cored and cut into quarters
- 1 tsp cinnamon
- 1/4 cup apple juice
- 2 apples, peeled, cored and diced

DIRECTIONS:

1. Put all of the ingredients in the inner pot of air fryer and stir well.
2. Seal pot and cook on high for 4 minutes.
3. As soon as the cooking is done, let it release pressure naturally. Remove lid.
4. Blend pear apple mixture using an immersion blender until smooth.
5. Serve and enjoy.

NUTRITION: Calories: 103 Protein: 0.6 g .Fat: 0.3 g. Carbs: 27.1 g.

95. Pear Sauce

Preparation Time: 10 minutes

Cooking Time: 15 minutes

Servings: 6

INGREDIENTS:

- 10 pears, sliced
- 1 cup apple juice
- 1 1/2 tsp cinnamon
- 1/4 tsp nutmeg

DIRECTIONS:

1. Put all of the ingredients in the air fryer and stir well.
2. Seal pot and cook on high for 15 minutes.
3. Once done, allow to release pressure naturally for 10 minutes then release remaining using quick release. Remove lid.
4. Blend the pear mixture using an immersion blender until smooth.
5. Serve and enjoy.

NUTRITION: Calories: 222 Protein: 1.3 g. Fat: 0.6 g. Carbs: 58.2 g.

96. Sweet Peach Jam

Preparation Time: 10 minutes

Cooking Time: 16 minutes

Servings: 20

INGREDIENTS:

- 1 1/2 lb fresh peaches, pitted and chopped

- 1/2 tbsp vanilla
- 1/4 cup maple syrup

DIRECTIONS:

1. Put all of the ingredients in the air fryer and stir well.
2. Seal pot and cook on high for 1 minute.
3. Once done, allow to release pressure naturally. Remove lid.
4. Set pot on sauté mode and cook for 15 minutes or until jam thickened.
5. Pour into the container and store it in the fridge.

NUTRITION: Calories: 16 Protein: 0.1 g. Fat: 0 g. Carbs: 3.7 g.

97. Warm Peach Compote

Preparation Time: 10 minutes

Cooking Time: 1 minute

Servings: 4

INGREDIENTS:

- 4 peaches, peeled and chopped
- 1 tbsp water
- 1/2 tbsp cornstarch
- 1 tsp vanilla

DIRECTIONS:

1. Add water, vanilla, and peaches into the air fryer basket.
2. Seal pot and cook on high for 1 minute.

3. Once done, allow to release pressure naturally. Remove lid.
4. In a small bowl, whisk together 1 tablespoon of water and cornstarch and pour into the pot and stir well.
5. Serve and enjoy.

NUTRITION: Calories: 66 Protein: 1.4 g. Fat: 0.4 g. Carbs: 15 g.

98. Spiced Pear Sauce

Preparation Time: 10 minutes

Cooking Time: 6 hours

Servings: 12

INGREDIENTS:

- 8 pears, cored and diced
- 1/2 tsp ground cinnamon
- 1/4 tsp ground nutmeg
- 1/4 tsp ground cardamom
- 1 cup of water

DIRECTIONS:

1. Put all of the ingredients in the air fryer and stir well.
2. Seal the pot with a lid and select slow cook mode and cook on low for 6 hours.
3. Mash the sauce using potato masher.
4. Pour into the container and store.

NUTRITION: Calories: 81 Protein: 0.5 g. Fat: 0.2 g. Carbs: 21.4 g.

99. Honey Fruit Compote

Preparation Time: 10 minutes

Cooking Time: 3 minutes

Servings: 4

INGREDIENTS:

- 1/3 cup honey
- 1 1/2 cups blueberries
- 1 1/2 cups raspberries

DIRECTIONS:

1. Put all of the ingredients in the air fryer basket and stir well.
2. Seal pot with lid and cook on high for 3 minutes.
3. Once done, allow to release pressure naturally. Remove lid.
4. Serve and enjoy.

NUTRITION: Calories: 141 Protein: 1 g. Fat: 0.5 g. Carbs: 36.7 g.

CONCLUSION

Power XL smokeless is another name for convenient, mess-free indoor grilling. This amazing grill has brought all the smart features that make grilling an effortless job. It's cost-effective and energy-efficient mechanism makes grilling a pleasing cooking experience. With a clear understanding of its basic features, functions, results, and safety measures, the device can prove to be a big relief for people who love to enjoy nicely flavored and evenly cooked food with a pleasing aroma. Now you don't need to set up a charcoal grill to enjoy the strong smoky flavorsyou can have it all by cooking your food right on your kitchen counter using the Power XL grill. So, stop waiting around, use our diverse collection of grilling recipes from this cookbook and start cooking some magic in this amazing smokeless electric grill at home. Cook the food of your choice with minimum effort and a lot more fun.

CPSIA information can be obtained
at www.ICGtesting.com
Printed in the USA
LVHW082258260121
677559LV00001B/5

9 781914 276989